The News in Egyptian Arabic

by Ahmad ElKhodary
with Matthew Aldrich

ISBN: 978-1-949650-26-6

Written by Ahmad ElKhodary

Edited by Matthew Aldrich

Audio by Ahmad ElKhodary

Photo Credits:

cover art © Can Stock Photo / Krisdog; p. 1 © Can Stock Photo / AlexAnton; p. 8 NASA; p. 15 © Can Stock Photo / Bialasiewicz; p. 22 © Can Stock Photo / ckellyphoto; p. 29 CC BY-SA 3.0 Pixabay / truthseeker08; p. 36 CC BY-SA 3.0 Wikipedia / PepedoCouto; p. 43 © eukonkanto.fi; p. 50 ; p. 57 © Matt Curnock; p. 64 CC BY-SA 3.0 Wikipedia / lienyuan lee; p. 71 © Can Stock Photo / dobled; p. 78 © Google; p. 85 CC BY-SA 3.0; p. 92 CC BY-SA 3.0; p. 99 © Can Stock Photo / petro; p. 106 CC BY-SA 3.0 Pixabay / Emilian Robert Vicol; p. 113 © Can Stock Photo / Razvanjp; p. 120 © Can Stock Photo / fxegs; p. 127 hieroglyphicsinitiative.ubisoft.com; p. 134 CC BY-SA 2.0 Pixabay / jessicadally; p. 141 CC BY-SA 3.0; p. 148 CC BY-ND 2.0 Pixabay / Rockin'Rita; p. 155 © Pizza Home; p. 162 © Can Stock Photo / 4774344sean; p. 169 © Can Stock Photo / LeonidAndronov

website: www.lingualism.com

email: contact@lingualism.com

المحتويات

القسم	العنوان	الصفحة
المقدمة		iii
إزاي تستعمل الكتاب ده		iv
الصفحة الأولى	مصر أحسن بلد تزورها في ٢٠٢٠	١
الطبيعة و البيئة	القطب الشمالي سجل أعلى درجة حرارة	٩
	الحشرات قلت ٢٧٪ في ٣٠ سنة	١٥٣
	برجر كينج بيغير نظام أكل البقر	١٦٩
	الحر الرهيب و الجفاف بيزودوا الحرايق الطبيعية في كاليفورنيا	١٩٣
الصحة و الأكل	دراسة: مراهقين أقل بيتعاطوا الماريجوانا لما بتتقنن	١٧
	فاكهة ريحتها قوية ودت ٦ أشخاص المستشفى	٣٣
	مدينة أسبانية عايزة تخس ١٠٠ ألف كيلو في سنتين	٤١
	دراسة: الأمريكان الأغنيا بيناموا أحسن من الفقرا	١٨٥
الاقتصاد و الشغل	البيوت الصغيرة جدا	٢٥
	معظم الأمريكان عايزين يشتغلوا من البيت	٨١
	فرنسا حولت النبيت اللي متباعش لمطهر إيد	١٣٧
	ممكن تجرب الـ"كورونا برجر"؟	١٧٧
الرياضة و الترفيه	راجل و مراته من ليتوانيا كسبوا مسابقة "شيل زوجات"	٤٩
	متحف فن تحت الماية فتح في أستراليا	٥٧
	چي كي رولينج نشرت كتاب جديد مجاني أونلاين	٩٧
	مركب و عجلة و بيت في نفس الوقت	١٠٥
العلم و التكنولوچيا	خاصية شورتس على يوتيوب هتنافس تيك توك	٨٩
	اكتشاف: بكتيريا جديدة بتاكل البلاستك	١٢١
	جوجل عملت تطبيق بيترجم الهيروغليفي	١٤٥
	جوانتي بيترجم لغة الإشارة لكلام	١٦١
أخبار مختلفة	أطفال أونتاريو هيتعلموا البرمجة و الإدارة المالية من سن ست سنين	٦٥
	مصر فتحت الهرم المنحني للزوار	٧٣
	دراسة: بدأ اليوم الدراسي متأخر أحسن	١١٣
	مدينة يابانية منعت الموبايل أثناء المشي	١٢٩

Table of Contents

Section	Title	Page
Introduction		iii
How to Use This Book		iv
Front Page	Egypt Is the Number One Country to...	1
Nature and Environment	Arctic Records Its Highest Temperature	9
	Insects Decrease by 27% in 30 Years	153
	Burger King Changes Cows' Diets	169
	Extreme Heat, Dry Weather Increase...	193
Health and Food	Study: Fewer Teens Consume Marijuana...	17
	Smelly Fruit Sends Six People to Hospital	33
	Spanish Town Wants to Lose 100,000 Kilos...	41
	Study: Rich Americans Sleep Better Than...	185
Economics and Business	Tiny Homes	25
	Most Americans Want to Continue...	81
	France Turns Unsold Wine Into Hand...	137
	Would You Try the 'Coronaburger'?	177
Sports and Leisure	Lithuanian Couple Wins Wife-Carrying...	49
	Museum of Underwater Art Opens in...	57
	J.K. Rowling Releases New Book Online...	97
	Boat, Bike and House at the Same Time	105
Science and Technology	'Shorts' Feature on YouTube to Compete...	89
	Discovery: New Bacteria Eats Plastic	121
	Google Makes Hieroglyphics Translator	145
	Gloves Translate Sign Language into...	161
Other News	Ontario Kids to Learn Coding and Finance...	65
	Egypt Opens Bent Pyramid to Visitors	73
	Study: Starting School Day Late is Better	113
	Japanese City Bans Phone Use While...	129

Introduction

In Egypt, as in other Arab countries, the news is published in Modern Standard Arabic (MSA). Of course, people don't discuss the news in MSA; we use Egyptian Arabic (Masri). And this is the guiding idea behind **The News in Egyptian Arabic**.

Matthew and I have created this book to help bridge the gap for intermediate and advanced learners who would like to understand and discuss a variety of more advanced topics that take you beyond everyday vocabulary in Egyptian Arabic.

This is also an attempt to demonstrate that Egyptian Arabic is more than just a "colloquial dialect" and that it is actually very practical for students of Arabic to learn even if their learning goals are more academic or formal.

The articles in this book were taken from real news stories in 2020 but were carefully chosen so that the topics would not quickly become dated and would be interesting and relevant for years to come. The units are organized to make them ideal study materials both for independent learners and those studying with a teacher, whether as online private lessons or in a classroom setting.

We hope you enjoy studying from this book as much as we enjoyed creating it, and we will be waiting for your valuable and constructive feedback.

Happy learning!

Ahmad ElKhodary

December 7, 2020

How to Use This Book

The book is made up of twenty-five units: a front-page article followed by twenty-four more articles grouped into six categories, as can be seen in the Table of Contents.

The Main Text

Each unit begins with its article laid out in a format mimicking a newspaper. As this version of the text does not contain diacritics (tashkeel), it presents a challenge and is the best place to start and end your study of a unit. Before you move on to the other sections of the unit, try reading the main text to see how much you understand and how well you can read the text aloud without the help of diacritics. Then read along while listening to the audio (see page vi for the link to the free audio files). After you have studied the article in more depth by completing the other sections of the unit, return to the main text and read it again. From time to time, as a review, you should return to previously studied units and read the main texts again.

Key Words

Several important words from the article are listed in the right-hand column. Irregular plurals of nouns and adjectives, as well as the imperfect form of verbs, are shown in parentheses. Each key word is followed by its definition in Arabic to help you work out the meaning of words that are new to you. Listen to the audio track for key words. If you feel the definitions are too challenging for your level, you can ignore them. After you have studied the key words, match them to their English translations that follow. You can easily match definitions for words you already know and then try to deduce the meaning of other key words through a process of elimination and other clues. You can find the answers in the Answer Key at the end of the unit. In the definitions, you may see the following terms:

- إسْم مفْعول (passive participle)
- المبْني لِلمجْهول (passive form [of a verb])
- عكْس (the opposite [of])

The Article

This section presents a version of the article augmented with tools to help you read and understand it better. The article is divided into numbered lines so you can match lines to their phonemic transcriptions and translations in the Answer Key. The text contains diacritics using the Lingualism system of orthography, which you can read more about on our website. (Navigate to The News in Egyptian Arabic → Resources Tab.) In Egyptian Arabic, ق is normally pronounced as a glottal stop (hamza). In some words, especially more academic (or formal) vocabulary, it is pronounced *q*. To help you with accurate pronunciation, in this book, we place a subtle wavy line under ق when it is pronounced *q*. Additionally, foreign names (of people, companies, cities, and regions–but not countries) appear **bold** to help you avoid confusion thinking they are Arabic words.

Comprehension and Discussion Questions

Following the article are three comprehension questions. You can find the answers by referring back to the article if needed. Five discussion questions provide ideas for discussion about the topic. If you are studying on your own, you are encouraged to answer them aloud or write your answers. English translations of the questions can be found in the Answer Key.

Expressions and Structures

This multiple-choice exercise helps you notice (and develop skills for noticing) how words work together in context and chunks of useful language. The English translations of four expressions or structures from the article are each followed by four choices in Arabic. One is correct, and three are either grammatically incorrect or do not match the translation. Take your time analyzing and comparing the choices before checking your answers in the Answer Key or searching for the answer in the article.

Answer Key and Translations

The Answer Key provides the answers to the Key Word matching exercise and the Expressions and Structures multiple-choice exercise. You can also find English translations of the article and the comprehension and discussion questions. {Curly brackets} show literal translations, while [square brackets] are necessary in English but are not present in the Arabic. There is also a version of the article in phonemic transcription to assist those who are not yet fully proficient in reading Arabic script for Egyptian Arabic and for those who want to analyze the pronunciation more closely. You can learn more about our phonemic transcription system on our website. (Navigate to The News in Egyptian Arabic → Resources Tab.) Note that, in this book, you will see some vowels in parentheses in the phonemic transcription. These vowels would normally elide (disappear) in fast, relaxed speech; however, because Ahmad is speaking in the audio at a very careful and slow pace, he pronounces these vowels. A schwa (ə) in parentheses, on the other hand, would be heard in relaxed speech, inserted to avoid three consonant sounds being pronounced in succession (a rule of Egyptian Arabic phonology); however, there is no schwa sound when a speaker pauses between words.

Notes

At the end of each unit is a lined section for taking notes, recording vocabulary, and/or writing out answers.

Visit the **News in Egyptian Arabic** hub at www.lingualism.com/nea, where you can find:

- **free accompanying audio** to download or stream (at variable playback rates)
- **guides** to the Lingualism orthographic (spelling and tashkeel) and phonemic transcription systems
- **links** to our Egyptian Arabic Facebook group and Ahmad's social media channels

الأخبار بالمصري

مصر أحسن بلد تزورها في ٢٠٢٠

مصر كانت أول بلد على قايمة البلاد اللي جرنال الإندپندنت اقترح إن الناس يزوروها في ٢٠٢٠.

المتحف المصري الكبير هيكون أكبر متحف أثري في العالم. المتحف هيكون فيه ٣٠ ألف قطعة أثرية جديدة.

الإندپندنت قال إن كان فيه حوالي ١١ مليون سايح في مصر في ٢٠١٨. الجرنال الإنجليزي برضه بيتوقع إن السياحة في مصر ترجع قوية تاني، بالذات بعد ما الطيران لشرم الشيخ اتفتح تاني، بعد ما كان اتقفل.

ناشونال چيوجرافيك برضه اختارت مدينة أسوان في مصر من ضمن المدن المقترحة في ٢٠٢٠.

بسبب كورونا، المتحف المصري الكبير هيفتح في ٢٠٢١. لكن الطيران اتفتح تاني في مصر، و سياح كتير بدأوا ييجوا مصر، بالذات لشرم الشيخ و الغردقة.

١

Egypt Is the Number One Country to Visit for 2020

Key Words — الكلمات

Study the key words and their definitions.

Translations	Definitions	Key Words
______	مجْموعةْ حاجات ليها علاقة ببعْض	قايْمة (قَوائِم)
______	إدّى رأْيُه	اِقْترح (يِقْترح)
______	شخْص زاير لِبلد أَوْ مدينة	سايِح / سايْحة (سُيّاح)
______	مجْموعةْ صفحات فيها أخْبار بِشكْل أساسي	جُرْنال (جرانيل)
______	خمّن حاجة هتِحْصل في المُسْتقْبل	اِتْوقع (يِتْوَقع)
______	زِيارةْ بلد أَوْ مدينة	سِياحة
______	مِش مسْموح بيه	ممْنوع

Now match these translations to the key words above. Check your answers in the answer key at the end of the unit.

banned • list • newspaper • to expect

to suggest • tourism • tourist

The Article — المقالة

1 مصْر أحْسن بلد تِزورْها في عِشْرين عِشْرين

2 مصْر كانِت أوِّل بلد على قايمْةْ البِلاد اللي جُرْنال **الإنْدِپِنْدِنْت** اِقْترح إنّ النّاس يِزوروها في عِشْرين عِشْرين.

3 المتْحف المصْري الكِّبير هَيْكون أكْبر متْحف أثري في العالم.

4 المتْحف هَيْكون فيه تلاتين ألْف قِطْعة أثرية جِديدة.

5 **الإنْدِپِنْدِنْت** قال إنّ كان فيه حَوالي حِداشر مِلْيوْن سايِح في مصْر في ألْفيْن و تمانْتاشر.

6 الجُرْنال الإنْجِليزي برْضُه بِيِتْوَقّع إنّ السِّياحة في مصْر تِرْجع قَوية تاني، بِالذّات بعْد ما الطَّيران لِشرْم الشّيْخ اِتْفتح تاني، بعْد ما كان اِتْقفل.

7 **ناشونال چيوجْرافيك** برْضُه اِخْتارِت مدينْةْ أسْوان في مصْر مِن ضِمْن المُدُن المُقْترحة في عِشْرين عِشْرين.

8 بِسبب كورونا، المتْحف المصْري الكِّبير هَيِفْتح في ألْفيْن واحِد و عِشْرين.

9 لكِن الطَيران اِتْفتح تاني في مصْر، و سُيّاح كتِير بدأوا ييجوا مصْر، بِالذّات لِشرْم الشّيْخ و الغرْدقة.

Comprehension Questions

١. **الإنْدِپِنْدِنْت** اِقْترح مدينِةْ أسْوان مِن ضِمْن المُدُن المقْترحة في ٢٠٢٠؟

٢. المتْحف المصْري الكِّبير هَيِفْتح إمْتى؟

٣. الطّيرَان لِشرْم الشّيْخ اِتْفتح وَلّا لِسّه؟

Discussion Questions أسئلة المناقشة

٤. أيْه رأْيَك في الخبر ده؟

٥. زُرْت مصْر قبْل كِده؟ لَوْ آه، شارِك تجْرُبْتك. لَوْ لأ، تِحِبّ تِزورْها؟

٦. زُرْت كام بلد في حَياتك؟

٧. أيْه التّغْيير اللي الكوروْنا عملِتُه في حَياتك؟

٨. أيْه أكْتر حاجة بِتْحِبّها في السّفر بِالطّيّارة؟

Expressions and Structures تعبيرات و تراكيب

Try to remember the Arabic expressions and structures from the article. Each English translation is followed by four choices, only one of which is correct. Refer back to the article to check your answers.

1. **the largest museum**

أكْبر المتْحف — الأكْبر متْحف

المتْحف الأكْتر كِبير — أكْبر متْحف

2. **eleven million tourists**

حِداشر مِلْيوْن السّايِح — حِداشر مِلْيوْن سايِح

حِداشر مِلْيوْنات مِن السُّيّاح — حِداشر مِلْيوْن سُيّاح

3. **especially**

بِالذّات — بِالظّبْط

بذاتًا — بِسبب

4. **because of**

لإِنّ — مِن سبب

عشان كِده — بِسبب

Answer Key and Translations

الإجابات و الترجمات

Key Word Answers

list قايْمة • to suggest اِقْترح • tourist سايِح • newspaper جُرْنال • to expect اِتْوَقّع • tourism سِياحة • banned ممْنوع

Translation of the Article

1. **Egypt Is the Number One Country to Visit for 2020**
2. Egypt was the first country on the list of countries that {the newspaper of} The Independent suggested people visit in 2020.
3. The Grand Egyptian Museum will be the largest archaeology museum in the world.
4. The museum will include thirty thousand new artifacts {archaeological pieces}.
5. The Independent said that there were about 11 million tourists in Egypt in 2018.
6. The English newspaper also expects that tourism in Egypt will return strong again, especially after flights {flying} to Sharm El-Sheikh have been resumed {opened again after it was closed}.
7. National Geographic also chose the city of Aswan in Egypt as one of the suggested cities in 2020.
8. Because of coronavirus, the Grand Egyptian Museum will open in 2021.
9. But flying has been resumed in Egypt, and many tourists have started coming to Egypt, especially to Sharm El-Sheikh and Hurghada.

Phonemic Transcription of the Article

1. *maṣr(ə) ʔáḫsan bálad tizúrha fi 3išrīn 3išrīn*
2. *maṣr(ə) kānit ʔáwwil bálad 3ála qáymit ilbilād ílli gurnāl il[Independent] iqtáraḫ inn innās yizurūha fi 3išrīn 3išrīn.*
3. *ilmátḫaf ilmáṣri -lkibīr haykūn ʔákbar mátḫaf ʔásari fi -l3ālam.*
4. *ilmátḫaf haykūn fī talatīn ʔalfə qíṭ3a ʔasaríyya g(i)dīda.*
5. *il[Independent] ʔāl innə kān fī ḫawāli ḫidāšar milyōn sāyiḫ fi maṣr fi ʔalfēn wi tamantāšar.*

6. *ilgurnāl ilʔingilīzi bárḍu biyatawáqqa3 inn issiyāɦa f maṣrə tírga3 qawíyya tāni, bi-zzāt ba3də ma -ṭṭayarān li-šarm iššēx itfátaɦ tāni, ba3də ma kān itʔáfal.*
7. *[National Geographic] bárḍu ixtārit madīnit ʔaswān fi maṣr min ḍimn ilmúdun ilmuqtáraɦa fi 3išrīn 3išrīn.*
8. *bi-sábab kurōna, ilmátɦaf ilmáṣri -lkibīr hayíftaɦ fi ʔalfēn wāɦid wi 3išrīn.*
9. *lākin iṭṭayarān itfátaɦ tāni fi maṣr, wi suyyāɦ kitīr bádaʔu yīgu maṣr, bi-zzāt li-šarm iššēx w ilɣardáʔa.*

Translation of the Questions

1. Did the Independent recommend Aswan among its recommended cities in 2020? 2. When will the Grand Egyptian Museum (GEM) open? 3. Have flights resumed yet? 4. What is your opinion of this news? 5. Have you visited Egypt before? If so, share your experience. If not, would you like to visit it? 6. How many countries have you visited in your life? 7. What changes has/did coronavirus make in your life? 8. What do you like most about traveling by plane?

Answers to Expressions and Structures

1. the largest museum أكْبر متْحف
2. eleven million tourists حِداشر مِليْون سايح
3. especially بِالذّات
4. because of بِسبب

Notes

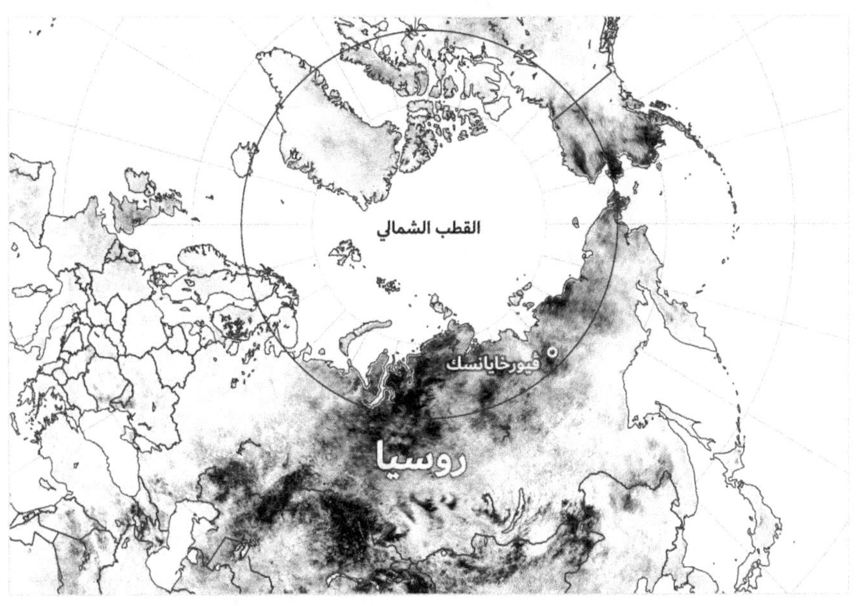

القطب الشمالي سجل أعلى درجة حرارة

مدينة ڤيورخايانسك في سيبيريا سجلت أعلى درجة حرارة في تاريخها، ٣٨°. ده رقم قياسي جديد. أعلى درجة حرارة اتسجلت في القطب الشمالي قبل كده كانت ٣٧.٢°.

درجة الحرارة بتزيد في القطب الشمالي بسرعة أسرع مرتين من بقية العالم.

مدينة ڤيورخايانسك دخلت موسوعة جينيس للأرقام القياسية بسبب الفرق الكبير بين أعلى و أقل درجة حرارة اتسجلوا هناك. أقل درجة حرارة اتسجلت فيها كانت -٦٨°. و أعلى درجة حرارة كانت ٣٧.٢° في سنة ١٩٨٨.

درجة الحرارة السنة دي، ٢٠٢٠، كانت عالية بشكل غريب في جزء كبير من سيبيريا. عشان كده، حصلت حرايق طبيعية كتير هناك.

٢

Arctic Records Its Highest Temperature

Key Words الكلمات

Study the key words and their definitions.

Translations	Definitions	Key Words
______	أكْتر مكان برْد شمال الأرْض	**القُطْب الشّمالي**
______	كتب مُلاحْظة	**سجِّل (يِسجِّل)**
______	المبْني للمجْهول مِن "سجِّل"	**اِتْسجِّل (يِتْسجِّل)**
______	رقم بيْقول الحاجة سُخْنة أَوْ بارْدة قدّ أيْه	**درجِةْ حرارة**
______	أعْلى رقم اِتْسجِّل	**رقم قِياسي (أرْقام قِياسية)**
______	بقى أكْتر	**زاد (يِزيد)**
______	كِتاب كِبير أوي فيه معْلومات كِتير	**مَوْسوعة**
______	الاِخْتِلاف بين حاجْتيْن أَوْ أكْتر	**فرْق (فُروق)**
______	نار كِتيرة بِتِحْصل في الغابات	**حريق طبيعي (حرايِق طبيعية)**

Now match these translations to the key words above. Check your answers in the answer key.

difference • encyclopedia • record • temperature • the Arctic • to be recorded • to increase • to record • wildfire

The Article المقالة

1 القُطْب الشّمالي سجِّل أعْلى درجِةْ حرارة

2 مدينِةْ **ڤْيورْخايانْسْك** في **سَيْبيرْيا** سجِّلِت أعْلى درجِةْ حرارة في تاريخْها، تمانْيَة و تلاتين درجة مِئَوية.

3 ده رقم قِياسي جِديد.

4 أعْلى درجِةْ حرارة اِتْسجِّلِت في القُطْب الشّمالي قبْل كِده كانِت سبْعة و تلاتين و اِتْنيْن مِن عشرة درجة مِئَوية.

5 درجِةْ الحرارة بِتْزيد في القُطْب الشّمالي بِسُرْعة أسْرع مرِّتيْن مِن بقيةْ العالم.

6 مدينِةْ **ڤْيورْخايانْسْك** دخلت مَوْسوعِةْ **جينيس** للأرْقام القِياسية بِسبب الفرْق الكِبير بيْن أعْلى و أقلّ درجِةْ حرارة اِتْسجِّلوا هِناك.

7 أقلّ درجِةْ حرارة اِتْسجِّلِت فيها كانِت سالِب تمانْيَة و سِتّين درجة مِئَوية.

8 و أعْلى درجِةْ حرارة كانِت سبْعة و تلاتين و اِتْنيْن مِن عشرة درجة مِئَوية في سنةْ ألْف تُسْعُمية تمانْيَة و تمانين.

9 درجِةْ الحرارة السّنة دي، عِشْرين عِشْرين، كانِت عالْيَة بِشكْل غريب في جُزْء كِبير مِن **سَيْبيرْيا**.

10 عشان كِده، حصلِت حرايِق طبيعية كِتير هِناك.

أسئلة الفهم Comprehension Questions

١. أيْه أقلّ درجِةْ حرارة اِتْسجِّلِت في مدينة **ڤْيورْخايانْسْك**؟

٢. درجِةْ الحرارة بِتْزيد في القُطْب الشّمالي بِسُرعة أقلّ مِن بقيِةْ العالم. صحّ وَلّا غلط؟

٣. ليه حصلت حرايق كتير في سيبيريا السنة دي؟

أسئلة المناقشة Discussion Questions

٤. أيْه رأْيَك في الخبر ده؟

٥. تِفْتِكِر تِقْدر تِعيش في مدينِة **ڤْيورْخايانْسْك**؟ ليْه؟

٦. حاسِس إنّ الصّيْف بقى حرّ أكْتر مِن زمان في بلدك؟ لَوْ آه، تِفْتِكِر أيْه السّبب؟

٧. بِتْحِبّ الحر ولا البرد؟ ليْه؟

٨. تِفْتِكِر أحسن جو في العالم موجود فين؟

Expressions and Structures تعبيرات و تراكيب

Try to remember the Arabic expressions and structures from the article. Each English translation is followed by four choices, only one of which is correct. Refer back to the article to check your answers.

1. **previously**

قبْل كِده — قبْلاً

قبْل ما — مِن قبْل

2. **the rest of the world**

ارْتاح العالم — بقيةْ العالم

العالم كُلُّه — العالم الفاضِل

3. **unusually**

على أشْكال غريبة — مِش عادةً

بِأغْرب شكْل — بِشكْل غريب

4. **because of that**

لإِنّ ده — عشان كِده

كذا سبب — بِسببٍ ما

Answer Key and Translations

الإجابات والترجمات

Key Word Answers

the Arctic القُطْب الشّمالي • to record سجِّل • to be recorded اِتْسجِّل • temperature درجة حرارة • record رقم • to increase زاد • encyclopedia مَوْسوعة • difference فرْق • wildfire حريق طبيعي

Translation of the Article

1. **Arctic Records Its Highest Temperature**
2. The city of Verkhoyansk in Siberia has recorded the highest temperature in its history–38°C.
3. This is a new record.
4. The highest temperature previously recorded in the Arctic was 37.2°C.
5. The temperature is increasing in the Arctic {with speed} two times faster than [in] the rest of the world.
6. The city of Verkhoyansk has entered the Guinness Book of World Records {the Encyclopedia of Guinness for Records} because of the big difference between the lowest and highest temperatures recorded there.
7. The lowest temperature recorded there {in it} [in Verkoyansk] was minus 68°C,
8. and the highest temperature was 37.2°C in {the year} 1988.
9. The temperature this year, 2020, was unusually high in a large part of Siberia.
10. Because of that, a lot of wildfires occurred there.

Phonemic Transcription of the Article

1. *ilʔúṭb iššamāli sággil ʔá3la dáragit ḫarāra*
2. *madīnit vyurxayánsk fi saybírya saggílit ʔá3la dáragit ḫarāra fi taríxha, tamánya wi talatīn dáraga miʔawíyya.*
3. *da ráqam qiyāsi g(i)dīd.*
4. *ʔá3la dáragit ḫarāra (i)tsaggílit fi -lʔuṭb iššamāli ʔablə kída kānit sáb3a w(i) talatīn w itnēn min 3ášara dáraga miʔawíyya.*

5. *dáragit ilɦarāra bitzīd fi -lʔuṭb iššamāli b(i)-súr3a ʔásra3 marritēn min baʔíyyit il3ālam.*
6. *madīnit vyurxayánsk dáxalit mawsū3it [Guiness] li-lʔarqām ilqiyasíyya b(i)-sábab ilfárʔ ilkibīr bēn ʔá3la wi ʔaʔállə dáragit ɦarāra (i)tsaggílu hināk.*
7. *ʔaʔállə dáragit ɦarāra (i)tsaggílit fīha kānit sālib tamánya w(i) sittīn dáraga miʔawíyya.*
8. *wi ʔá3la dáragit ɦarāra kānit sáb3a w(i) talatīn w itnēn min 3ášara dáraga miʔawíyya fi sánat ʔalfə tus3umíyya tamánya w(i) tamanīn.*
9. *dáragit ilɦarāra -ssanādi, 3išrīn 3išrīn, kānit 3ályа b(i)-šáklə ɣarīb fi guzʔə kbīr min saybírya.*
10. *3ašān kída, ɦáṣalit ɦarāyiʔ ṭabi3íyya k(i)tīr hināk.*

Translation of the Questions

1. What was the lowest temperature recorded in the city of Verkhoyansk? 2. The temperature in the Arctic is increasing faster than in the rest of the world? True or false? 3. Why did a lot of forest fires occur in Siberia this year? 4. What is your opinion on this news? 5. Do you think you could live in the city of Verkhoyansk? Why? 6. Do you think summer has become hotter than it used to be in your country? If so, what do you think is the reason? 7. Do you like the heat or the cold? Why? 8. Where do you think the best weather/climate in the world is?

Answers to Expressions and Structures

1. previously قبْل كِده
2. the rest of the world بقيْة العالم
3. unusually بِشكْل غريب
4. because of that عشان كِده

Notes

دراسة: مراهقين أقل بيتعاطوا الماريجوانا لما بتتقنن

فيه دراسة جديدة بتقول إن تقنين الماريجوانا الترفيهية للكبار احتمال يكون قلل تعاطي المراهقين ليها في بعض الولايات الأمريكية.

فيه ولايات كتير قننت الماريجوانا الطبية و الترفيهية.

مكانش فيه فرق كبير ليه علاقة بتقنين الماريجوانا الطبية. بس تعاطي المراهقين قل حوالي ١٠٪ بعد تقنين الماريجوانا الترفيهية.

الماريجوانا بتكون أصعب و أغلى على المراهقين إنهم يشتروها من أماكن مترخص لها إنها تبيع الماريجوانا. ده ممكن يكون سبب من الأسباب.

فيه دراسات تانية لقت إن مراهقين أقل بيفكروا إن الماريجوانا خطر لما بتكون قانونية للكبار.

٢٠٪ من طلاب الثانوي في أمريكا بيقولوا إنهم بيتعاطوا الماريجوانا.

Study: Fewer Teens Consume Marijuana When Legalized

Key Words الكلمات

Study the key words and their definitions.

Translations	Definitions	Key Words
______	أسْلوب مُنظّم في جمْع المعْلومات	دِراسة
______	إنّك تِخلّي حاجة قانونية؛ إنّك تِخلّي حاجة مِش ضِدّ القانون	تقنين
______	بالغ؛ مِش طِفْل	كِبير / كِبيرة (كْبار)
______	خلّى حاجة تِبْقى قُليِّلة	قَلِّل (يِقلِّل)
______	إنّك تاخُد مُخدّرات	تعاطي
______	شخْص عُمْرُه بين ١٣ و ١٩ سنة	مُراهِق / مراهْقة
______	منْطقة إدارية كِبيرة: فيه خمْسين وِلايَة في أمْريكا.	وِلايَة
______	بقى أصْغر في العدد، المساحة، الوَزْن، إلخ.	قَلّ (يِقِلّ)
______	لِلعِلاج	طِبّي
______	علشان المتْعة	ترْفيهي
______	عنْدُه رُخْصة	مِترْخّص لُه / لها (لُهُم)

Now match these translations to the key words on the previous page. Check your answers in the answer key.

adult • legalization • licensed • medical, medicinal • recreational • state • study • taking drugs • teenager • to decrease, become less • to reduce, decrease

The Article المقالة

1 دِراسة: مُراهْقين أقلّ بيِتْعاطوا الماريجْوانا لمّا بِتِتْقنّن

2 فيه دِراسة جِديدة بِتْقول إنّ تقْنين الماريجْوانا التّرْفيهية لِلكُبار اِحْتِمال يِكون قَلِّل تعاطي المُراهْقين ليها في بعْض الوِلايات الأمْريكية.

3 فيه وِلايات كِتير قِنِّنت الماريجْوانا الطِّبّية و التّرْفيهية.

4 مكانْش فيه فرْق كِبير ليه عِلاقة بِتقْنين الماريجْوانا الطِّبّية.

5 بسّ تعاطي المُراهْقين قلّ حَوالي عشرة في المية بعْد تقْنين الماريجْوانا التّرْفيهية.

6 الماريجْوانا بِتْكون أصْعب و أغْلى على المُراهْقين إنُّهْم يِشْترِوها مِن أماكِن مِتْرخّص لها إنّها تِبيع الماريجْوانا.

7 ده مُمْكِن يِكون سبب مِن الأسْباب.

8 فيه دِراسات تانْيَة لقِت إنّ مُراهْقين أقلّ بِيفكّروا إنّ الماريجْوانا خطر لمّا بِتْكون قانونية لِلكُبّار.

9 عِشْرين في المية مِن طُلّاب الثّانَوي في أمْريكا بِيْقولوا إنُّهْم بِيِتْعاطوا الماريجْوانا.

Comprehension Questions أسئلة الفهم

١. تعاطي المُراهْقين لِلماريجْوانا قلّ بعْد تقْنين الماريجْوانا الطِّبّية؟

٢. كام في المية مِن طُلّاب الثّانَوي في أمْريكا بِيْقولوا إنُّهُم بيِتْعاطوا ماريجْوانا؟

٣. هل الماريجْوانا بتِكون أسْهل و أرْخص في الأماكِن اللي مِترَخّص لها إنّها تِبيع ماريجْوانا؟

أسئلة المناقشة Discussion Questions

٤. أيْه رأْيَك في الدِّراسة دي؟

٥. تِفْتِكِر أيْه سبب إنّ تعاطي المُراهْقين لِلماريجْوانا بيِقِلّ لمّا بتِكون قانونية؟

٦. كان فيه طُلّاب كِتير في المدْرسة بِتاعْتك بيِتْعاطوا ماريجْوانا؟

٧. هتِعْمِل أيْه لَوْ عِرِفْت إنّ إبْنك المُراهِق بيِتْعاطى ماريجْوانا أَوْ بيِشْرب حشيش؟

٨. رأْي النّاس في بلدك في الماريجْوانا و الحشيش اِتْغيّر في خِلال الكام سنة اللي فاتوا وَلّا لأ؟

Expressions and Structures تعبيرات و تراكيب

Try to remember the Arabic expressions and structures from the article. Each English translation is followed by four choices, only one of which is correct. Refer back to the article to check your answers.

1. **there was not**

كان فيه | مكانْش فيه
هِناك مكانْش | كان مِش فيه

2. **one of the reasons**

واحِد سبب | السّبب مِن الأسْباب
سبب مِن السّبب | سبب مِن الأسْباب

3. **other studies have found that...**

فيه دِراسة تانْيين لقوا إنّ | فيه دِراسات تانْيَة لقِت إنّ
الدِّراسات التّانْيَة لقِت إنّ | فيه دِراسة تانْي لقِت إنّ

4. **twenty percent of**

عِشْرين مية | عِشْرون بِالمية مِن
عِشْرين في المية مِن | عشرات في مية مِن

Answer Key and Translations

الإجابات و الترجمات

Key Word Answers

study دِراسة • legalization تقنين • adult كبير • to reduce, decrease قَلِّل • taking drugs تعاطي • teenager مُراهِق • state وِلايَة • to decrease, become less قَلّ • medical, medicinal طِبّي • recreational ترْفيهي • licensed مِترْخّص له

Translation of the Article

1. **Study: Fewer Teens Consume Marijuana When Legalized**
2. {There is} a new study [that] says that legalizing recreational marijuana for adults may have reduced teens' consumption of it in some American states.
3. {There are} many states {that} have legalized medicinal and recreational marijuana.
4. There was not a big difference associated with legalizing medical marijuana.
5. However, the consumption by teens decreased [by] about 10% after legalizing recreational marijuana.
6. Marijuana is more difficult and expensive for teens to buy from places licensed to sell marijuana.
7. This could be one of the reasons.
8. Other studies have found that fewer teens think that marijuana is dangerous when it is legal for adults.
9. Twenty percent of high school students in the US say that they consume marijuana.

Phonemic Transcription of the Article

1. *dirāsa: murahqīn ʔaʔáll(ə) b(i)yit3āṭu -lmarigwāna lámma b(i)titqánnin*
2. *fī dirāsa g(i)dīda bitʔūl ʔinnə taqnīn ilmarigwāna (i)ttarfihíyya li-lkubār iḫtimāl yikūn ʔállil ta3āṭi -lmurahqīn līha fi ba3ḍ ilwilayāt ilʔamrikíyya.*
3. *fī wilayāt kitīr qannínit ilmarigwāna (i)ṭṭibbíyya w ittarfihíyya.*
4. *ma-kánšə fī farʔə k(i)bīr lī 3ilāqa b(i)-taqnīn ilmarigwāna -ṭṭibbíyya.*

5. *bassə ta3āṭi (i)lmurahqīn ʔall(ə) ɦawāli 3ášara fi -lmíyya ba3də taqnīn ilmarigwāna (i)ttarfihíyya.*
6. *ilmarigwāna bitkūn ʔáṣ3ab wi ʔáɣla 3ála -lmurahqīn ʔinnúhum yištirūha min ʔamākin mitraxxaṣ-láha ʔinnáha tibī3 ilmarigwāna.*
7. *da múmkin yikūn sábab min ilʔasbāb.*
8. *fī dirasāt tánya láʔit ʔinnə murahqīn ʔaʔáll(ə) biyfakkáru ʔinn ilmarigwāna xáṭar lámma bitkūn qanuníyya li-lkubār.*
9. *3išrīn fi -lmíyya min ṭullāb issānawi f(i) ʔamrīka biyʔūlu ʔinnúhum biyit3āṭu -lmarigwāna.*

Translation of the Questions

1. Did teens' consumption of marijuana decrease after the legalization of medicinal marijuana? 2. What percentage of high school students in the US say they use marijuana? 3. Does marijuana become easier [to buy] and cheaper in places that are licensed to sell marijuana? 4. What is your opinion of this study? 5. What do you think is the reason that teens' consumption of marijuana decreases when it becomes legal? 6. Were there a lot of students in your school that used marijuana? 7. What would you do if you found out that your teenage son was using marijuana or smoking hashish? 8. Have the views of people in your country on marijuana changed over the last several years?

Answers to Expressions and Structures

1. there was not مكانْش فيه
2. one of the reasons سبب مِن الأسْباب
3. other studies have found that... فيه دِراسات تانْيَة لقِت إنّ
4. twenty percent of عِشْرين في المية مِن

Notes

البيوت الصغيرة جدا

البيوت الصغيرة جدا–٤٠ متر مربع أو أقل– بقت موضة في الكام سنة اللي فاتوا. حوالي نص الأمريكان بيقولوا إنهم ممكن يفكروا يشتروا واحد.

البيوت الصغيرة جدا من جوه بتكون زي البيوت العادية، بس أصغر؛ يعني بيكون فيه مطبخ أمريكاني و صالة و حمام. و بيكون طبعا فيه سرير. معظم البيوت دي بتكون مبنية على مقطورات عشان الناس يقدروا يغيروا أماكنهم بسهولة.

أسعار البيوت الصغيرة جدا عادة بتكون أقل من ربع أسعار البيوت العادية.

بعض الناس بيحبوا البيوت الصغيرة جدا عشان البيوت دي صديقة للبيئة.

فيه ناس بيقولوا إن البيوت دي خيار كويس جدا للشباب. ده لإن الشباب بيكونوا عايزين مكان يعيشوا فيه، بس مش دايما بيكون عندهم فلوس عشان يشتروا أرض يبنوا عليها بيت عادي.

٤ Tiny Homes

Key Words

الكلمات

Study the key words and their definitions.

Translations	Definitions	Key Words
____________	مِساحةْ مُربّع طول ضِلْعُه مِترْ واحِد	مِترْ مُربّع
____________	حاجة مُنْتشِرة؛ ناس كِتير بيِعْمِلوها أَوْ بيِتْكلِّموا عنْها	موْضة
____________	عربية مفيهاش موتوْر بتِتْجرّ بِعربية تانْيَة	مقْطورة
____________	كُوَيِّس لِلبيئة	صديق لِلبيئة
____________	حاجة مُمْكِن تِخْتارْها	خِيار
____________	عمل مبْنى	بنى (يِبْني)

Now match these translations to the key words above. Check your answers in the answer key.

environmentally friendly • option •
square meter • to build • trailer • trend

The Article

المقالة

1 البُيوت الصُّغيّرة جِدّاً

2 البُيوت الصُّغيّرة جِدّاً-أرْبِعين مِتر مُربّع أَوْ أقلّ-بقِت موْضة في الكام سنة اللي فاتوا.

3 حَوالي نُصّ الأمْريكان بِيْقولوا إنُّهْم مُمْكِن يِفكّروا يِشْترِوا واحِد.

4 البُيوت الصُّغيّرة جِدّاً مِن جُوّه بِتْكون زيّ البُيوت العادية، بسّ أصْغر؛

5 يَعْني بِيْكون فيه مطْبخ أمْريكاني و صالة و حمّام.

6 و بِيْكون طبْعاً فيه سِرير.

7 مُعْظم البُيوت دي بِتْكون مبْنية على مقْطورات عشان النّاس يِقْدروا يِغيرّوا أماكِنْهُم بِسْهولة.

8 أسْعار البُيوت الصُّغيّرة جِدّاً عادةً بِتْكون أقلّ مِن رُبْع أسْعار البُيوت العادية.

9 بعْض النّاس بِيْحِبّوا البُيوت الصُّغيّرة جِدّاً عشان البُيوت دي صديقة لِلبيئة.

10 فيه ناس بِيْقولوا إنّ البُيوت دي خِيار كُوَيِّس جِدّاً لِلشّباب.

11 ده لإِنّ الشّباب بِيْكونوا عايْزين مكان يِعيشوا فيه، بسّ مِش دايْماً بِيْكون عنْدُهْم فِلوس عشان يِشْترِوا أرْض يِبْنوا عليْها بيْت عادي.

أسئلة الفهم Comprehension Questions

١. أيْه هِيَّ البُيوت الصُّغيرّة جِدّاً؟

٢. البُيوت الصُّغيرّة جِدّاً بِتْكون أرْخص قدّ أيْه مِن البُيوت العادية؟

٣. ليْه البُيوت الصُّغيرّة جِدّاً مُمْكِن تِكون خِيار كُوَيِّس لِلشّباب؟

أسئلة المناقشة Discussion Questions

٤. أيْه رأْيَك في المقالة دي؟

٥. تِفْتِكِر مُمْكِن تِشْترِي بيْت صُغيرّ جِدّاً؟

٦. فيه بُيوت صُغيرّة جِدّاً في مدينْتك؟

٧. تِفضّل تِبْني بيْتك بِنفْسك وَلّا تِشْترِي بيْت معْمول جاهِز؟

٨. أيْه أهمّ حاجة بِالنِّسْبة لك لمّا تيجي تِشْترِي أَوْ تِأجّر بيْت؟

Expressions and Structures تعبيرات و تراكيب

Try to remember the Arabic expressions and structures from the article. Each English translation is followed by four choices, only one of which is correct. Refer back to the article to check your answers.

1. **in the last few years**

في الكام سنة اللي فاتوا	في كام السّنة اللي فاتوا
في شْوَيّة سِنين اللي فاتِت	في الكام سِنين اللي فاتوا

2. **most of these houses**

المُعْظم مِن البُيوت دي	كُلّ البُيوت دي
مُعْظم البُيوت دي	البُيوت العظيمة دي

3. **less than**

على الأقلّ	أقلّ مِن
الأقلّ مِن	أقلّ في

4. **some people say...**

فيه ناس بِيْقولوا	بعْض النّاس بِيْحِبّوا
النّاس تِيْقول	بعْضُهْم مِن النّاس بِيْقول

Answer Key and Translations الإجابات و الترجمات

Key Word Answers

square meter مِتر مُربّع • trend موْضة • trailer مقْطورة • environmentally friendly صديق لِلبيئة • option خِيار • to build بنى

Translation of the Article

1. **Tiny Homes**
2. "Tiny Homes"–40 square meters or less–have become a trend in the last few years.
3. About half of Americans say that they may consider buying one.
4. Tiny homes, from the inside, are like regular houses but smaller.
5. That is, they have an open-plan kitchen {American kitchen}, a living area, and a bathroom.
6. And they have a bed, of course.
7. Most of these houses are built on trailers so that people can change their locations easily.
8. The prices of tiny homes are usually less than a quarter of the prices of traditional houses.
9. Some people like tiny homes because these houses are environmentally friendly.
10. Some people say that these houses are a very good option for young people.
11. This is because young people will want a place to live in, but not always do they have money to buy land to build a regular house on.

Phonemic Transcription of the Article

1. *ilbuyūt iṣṣuɣayyára gíddan*
2. *ilbuyūt iṣṣuɣayyára giddan–ʔarbi3īn mítrə murábba3 ʔaw ʔaʔall–báʔit mōḍa fi -lkām sána ílli fātu.*
3. *ɧawāli nuṣṣ ilʔamrikān biyʔūlu ʔinnúhum múmkin yifakkáru yištíru wāɧid.*
4. *ilbuyūt iṣṣuɣayyára gíddan min gúwwa bitkūn zayy ilbuyūt il3adíyya, bassə ʔaṣɣar;*

5. *yá3ni biykūn fī máţbax ʔamrikāni wi şāla wi ħammām.*
6. *wi biykūn ţáb3an fī srīr.*
7. *mú3ẓam ilbuyūt di bitkūn mabníyya 3ála maʔţurāt 3ašān innās yiʔdáru yiɣayyáru ʔamakínhum bi-shūla.*
8. *ʔas3ār ilbuyūt işşuɣayyára gíddan 3ādatan bitkūn ʔaʔáll(ə) min rub3ə ʔas3ār ilbuyūt il3adíyya.*
9. *ba3ḍ innās biyħíbbu -lbuyūt işşuɣayyára gíddan 3ašān ilbuyūt di şadīqa li-lbīʔa.*
10. *fī nās biyʔūlu ʔinn ilbuyūt di xiyār kuwáyyis gíddan li-ššabāb.*
11. *da li-ʔinn iššabāb biykūnu 3ayzīn makān yi3īšu fī, bassə miš dáyman biykūn 3andúhum filūs 3ašān yištíru ʔarḍ(ə) yíbnu 3alēha bēt 3ādi.*

Translation of the Questions

1. What are tiny homes? 2. How much cheaper are tiny homes than regular houses? 3. Why might tiny homes be a good option for young people? 4. What is your opinion of this article? 5. Would you consider buying a tiny home? 6. Are there tiny homes in your town? 7. Would you prefer to build a house yourself or buy a house ready-made? 8. What is the most important thing for you when you go to buy or rent a house?

Answers to Expressions and Structures

1. in the last few years في الكام سنة اللي فاتوا
2. most of these houses مُعْظم البُيوت دي
3. less than أقلّ مِن
4. some people say... فيه ناس بِيْقولوا

Notes

فاكهة ريحتها قوية ودت ٦ أشخاص المستشفى

٦ موظفين في مكتب بوسطة في ألمانيا راحوا المستشفى بعد ما لقوا شحنة ريحتها قوية جدا. الشحنة كان فيها فاكهة الدوريان.

لما البوليس و المطافي جم عشان يشوفوا الشحنة، كانوا خايفين إنها تكون فيها حاجة خطر. و عشان كده، البوليس فضى المبنى كله و طلب من كل الموظفين إنهم يمشوا. ٦ عربيات إسعاف و ٧ عربيات طوارئ جم كمان عشان يساعدوا.

الدوريان كان رايح لراجل عنده ٥٠ سنة في المنطقة. الراجل استلم الشحنة بتاعته في الآخر.

فيه ناس بيقولوا على الدوريان "ملك الفاكهة". و فيه ناس بيقولوا إن ريحته زي ريحة البيض البايظ أو الجبنة البايظة أو الشرابات الوسخة. عشان كده، الدوريان ممنوع في فنادق كتير و حتى في مترو سنغافورة.

٥ Smelly Fruit Sends Six People to Hospital

Key Words

الكلمات

Study the key words and their definitions.

Key Words	Definitions	Translations
مكْتب بوسْطة (مكاتِب بوسْطة)	مكْتب بريد	__________
مُوَظّف / مُوَظّفة	عامِل	__________
شُحْنَة	حاجة مبْعوتة مِن مكان لِمكان	__________
ريحَة (رَوايِح)	حاجة مُمْكِن نِشِمّها	__________
خَطر	مِش أمان	__________
بايِظ	مِش سليم	__________
شُراب	الحاجة اللي بِنِلْبِسْها في رِجْليْنا قبْل ما نِلْبِس الجزْمة	__________
وِسِخ	مِش نضيف	__________
فضّى (يِفضّي)	خلّى حاجة تِبْقى فاضْيَة	__________
عربيةْ إسْعاف	عربية بِتْوَدّي العيّانين المُسْتشْفى	__________
عربيةْ طَوارِئ	عربية بِتيجي لمّا يِكون فيه مُشْكِلة كِبيرة	__________

Now match these translations to the key words above. Check your answers in the answer key.

a pair of socks • ambulance • dangrous • dirty • emergency vehicle • employee • post office • rotten, spoiled • shipment • smell • to empty, evacuate

The Article المقالة

1 فاكْهة ريحِتْها قَوية وَدِّت سِتّ أشْخاص المُسْتشْفى

2 سِتّ مُوَظّفين في مكْتب بوسْطة في ألْمانْيا راحوا المُسْتشْفى بعْد ما لقوا شُحْنة ريحِتْها قَوية جِدّاً.

3 الشُّحْنة كان فيها فاكْهِةْ الدّوريان.

4 لمّا البوليس و المطافي جُم عشان يِشوفوا الشُّحْنة، كانوا خايْفين إنّها تِكون فيها حاجة خطر.

5 و عشان كِده، البوليس فضّى المبْنى كُلُّه و طلب مِن كُلّ المُوَظّفين إنُّهْم يِمْشوا.

6 سِتّ عربيات إسْعاف و سبع عربيات طَوارِئ جُم كمان عشان يِساعْدوا.

7 الدّوريان كان رايِح لِراجِل عنْدُه خمْسين سنة في المنْطِقة.

8 الرّاجِل اِسْتلم الشُّحْنة بِتاعْتُه في الآخِر.

9 فيه ناس بِيْقولوا على الدّوريان "ملِك الفاكْهة".

10 و فيه ناس بِيْقولوا إنّ ريحْتُه زيّ ريحِةْ البيْض البايِظ أَوْ الجِبْنة البايْظة أَوْ الشُّرابات الوِسْخة.

11 عشان كِده، الدّوريان ممْنوع في فنادِق كِتير و حتّى في مِتْرو سِنْغافورة.

أسئلة الفهم Comprehension Questions

١. كام مُوَظّف دخل المُسْتشْفى؟

٢. البوليس عمل أيْه؟

٣. الدّورِيان كان رايِح لِمين؟

أسئلة المناقشة Discussion Questions

٤. أيْه رأْيَك في المقالة دي؟

٥. أيْه أغْرب حاجة أكلْتها قبْل كِده؟

٦. بِتْحِبّ تِجرّب أكلات جِديدة؟

٧. لَوْ هتاكُل أكْلة واحْدة كُلّ يوْم، هتِخْتار أيْه؟

٨. لَوْ لازِم تِخْتار تِشْتغل في مكْتب بوسْطة أَوْ قِسْم شُرْطة أَوْ في مُسْتشْفى، هتِخْتار أيْه و ليْه؟

Expressions and Structures تعبيرات و تراكيب

Try to remember the Arabic expressions and structures from the article. Each English translation is followed by four choices, only one of which is correct. Refer back to the article to check your answers.

1. **six employees**

سِتّة مُوَظّف — سِتّة مُوظّفين

سِتّ مُوَظّفين — سِتّ مُوَظّف

2. **something dangerous**

حاجة خطر — خطر الحاجة

حاجة خطرة — حاجة خاطْرة

3. **a 50-year-old man**

راجِل اللي عنْدُه خمْسين سِنين — راجِل مِن خمْسين سنة

الراجِل اللي عنْدُه خمْسين سنة — راجِل عنْدُه خمْسين سنة

4. **in many hotels**

في الفنادِق كتيرة — فيه فنادِق كتيرة

في كِتير فنادِق — في فنادِق كِتير

Answer Key and Translations الإجابات و الترجمات

Key Word Answers

post office مكْتب بوسْطة • employee مُوَظّف • shimpent شُحْنَة • smell ريحَة • dangrous خَطر • rotten, spoiled بايِظ • a pair of socks شُراب • dirty وِسِخ • to empty فضّى • ambulance عربيةْ إسْعاف • emergency vehicle عربيةْ طَوارِئ

Translation of the Article

1. **Smelly Fruit Sends Six People to Hospital**
2. Six employees in a post office in Germany went to the hospital after they found a package whose smell was strong.
3. The package included durian fruits.
4. When the police and fire department came to see the package, they were afraid that it might have something dangerous.
5. Therefore, the police evacuated the whole building and asked all the employees to leave.
6. Six ambulances {aid cars} and seven emergency cars came as well to help.
7. The durians were going to a 50-year-old man in the neighborhood.
8. The man received his package in the end.
9. Some people refer to durians as {say about the durian} the King of Fruits.
10. And some say that its smell is like the smell of rotten eggs, spoiled cheese, or dirty socks.
11. Durians are not allowed in many hotels and even in the subway of Singapore.

Phonemic Transcription of the Article

1. *fákha riɧítha qawíyya wáddit sittə ʔašxāṣ ilmustášfa*
2. *sittə muwaẓẓafīn fi máktab búsṭa fi ʔalmánya rāɧu -lmustášfa ba3də ma láʔu šúɧna riɧítha qawíyya gíddan.*
3. *iššúɧna kān fīha fákhit iddūriyan.*
4. *lámma -lbulīs w ilmaṭāfi gum 3ašān yišūfu -ššúɧna, kānu xayfīn ʔinnáha t(i)kūn fīha ɧāga xáṭar.*

5. *wi 3ašān kída, ilbulīs fáḍḍa (i)lmábna kúllu wi ṭálab min kull ilmuwaẓẓafīn ʔinnúhum yímšu.*
6. *sittə 3arabiyyāt ʔis3āf wi sába3 3arabiyyāt ṭawāriʔ gum kamān 3ašān yisá3du.*
7. *iddūriyan kān rāyiḥ li-rāgil 3ándu xamsīn sána fi -lmanṭíʔa.*
8. *irrāgil istálam iššúḥna b(i)tá3tu fi -lʔāxir.*
9. *fī nās biyʔūlu 3ála -ddūriyan "málik ilfákha".*
10. *wi fī nās biyʔūlu ʔinnə ríḥtu zayyə rīḥit ilbēḍ ilbāyiẓ ʔaw ilgíbna ilbáyẓa ʔaw iššurabāt ilwísxa.*
11. *3ašān kída, iddūriyan mamnū3 fi fanādiʔ kitīr wi ḥátta f(i) mítru sinɣafūra.*

Translation of the Questions

1. How many employees went to the hospital? 2. What did the police do? 3. Who was the durian going to? 4. What is your opinion of this article? 5. What is the strangest thing you have ever eaten? 6. Do you like trying new foods? 7. If you were going to eat the same food every day, what would you choose? 8. If you had to work in a post office, police station, or in a hospital, what would you choose and why?

Answers to Expressions and Structures

1. six employees سِتّ مُوَظّفين
2. something dangerous حاجة خطر
3. a 50-year-old man راجِل عنْدُه خمْسين سنة
4. in many hotels في فنادِق كتير

Notes

مدينة أسبانية عايزة تخس ١٠٠ ألف كيلو في سنتين

فيه تحدي في مدينة نارون الأسبانية إن سكانها يخسوا ١٠٠ ألف كيلو كمجموعة في سنتين.

ترجمة إسم التحدي بالأسباني هي: ١٠٠ ألف سبب للوزن. التحدي بدأ في يناير ٢٠١٨، و بعد سنة الناس كانوا خسوا ٤٦ ألف كيلو.

عدد سكان نارون ٣٩ ألف شخص؛ يعني كل شخص هناك لازم يخس حوالي كيلو و نص في سنتين عشان المدينة تخس ١٠٠ ألف كيلو.

إدارة الصحة هناك قالت إن فيه ١٥ ألف شخص محتاج يخس في المدينة. الهدف إن الناس دول يخسوا على الأقل ١٠٪ من وزنهم.

فيه جمعية خيرية في المدينة هتتبرع بأكل أو لبن لأفقر ناس في المدينة لكل كيلو الناس هيخسوه.

Spanish Town Wants to Lose 100,000 Kilos in Two Years

Key Words الكلمات

Study the key words and their definitions.

Translations	Definitions	Key Words
________	دعْوَة لِلمُشارْكة في مُنافْسة	تحدّي
________	شخْص عايِش في مكان	ساكِن / ساكْنَة (سُكّان)
________	وَزْنُه قلّ	خسّ (يِخِسّ)
________	قِسْم في الحُكومة، شِرْكة، إلخ.، ليه مسْؤولية مُعيّنة	إدارة
________	الحدّ الأدْنى	على الأقلّ
________	حاجة عايِز تِوْصلّها	هدف (أهْداف)
________	شِرْكة مِش هدفْها الفِلوس	جمْعية خيْرية
________	إدّى حاجة مِن غيْر مُقابِل مادّي	اِتْبرّع (يِتْبرّع)

Now match these translations to the key words above. Check your answers in the answer key.

administration • at least • challenge • charity •
goal • resident • to donate • to lose weight

The Article المقالة

1 مدينة أسْبانية عايْزة تِخِسّ مية ألْف كيلو في سنتيْن

2 فيه تحدّي في مدينةْ **نارْوْن** الأسْبانية إنّ سُكّانْها يِخِسّوا مية ألْف كيلو كمجْموعة في سنتيْن.

3 ترْجمِة إسْمِ التّحدّي بِالأسْباني هِيَّ: مية ألْف سبب لِلوَزْن.

4 التّحدّي بدأ في يَنايِر ألْفيْن و تمانْتاشر، و بعْد سنة النّاس كانوا خسّوا سِتّة و أرْبِعين ألْف كيلو.

5 عدد سُكّان **نارْوْن** تِسْعة و تلاتين ألْف شخْص؛

6 يَعْني كُلّ شخْص هِناك لازِم يِخِسّ حَوالي كيلو و نُصّ في سنتيْن عشان المدينة تِخِسّ مية ألْف كيلو.

7 إدارةْ الصِّحّة هِناك قالِت إنّ فيه خمسْتاشر ألْف شخْص مِحْتاج يِخِسّ في المدينة.

8 الهدف إنّ النّاس دوْل يِخِسّوا على الأقلّ عشرة في المية مِن وَزْنُهْم.

9 فيه جمْعية خَيْرِية في المدينة هتِتْبرّع بِأكْل أَوْ لبن لِأفْقر ناس في المدينة لِكُلّ كيلو النّاس هَيْخِسّوه.

أسئلة الفهم Comprehension Questions

١. عدد سُكّان مدينةْ **نارون** قدّ أيْه؟

٢. فيه كام شخْص مِحْتاج يِخِسّ؟

٣. الجمْعية الخَيْرية اللي في المدينة هتِعْمِل أيْه؟

أسئلة المناقشة Discussion Questions

٤. أيْه رأْيَك في الخبر ده؟

٥. الوَزْن مُشْكِلة كِبيرة في مدينْتك؟

٦. في رأْيك، الرِّياضة أهمّ وَلّا الأكْل الصِّحّي؟ ليْه؟

٧. أيْه أكْتر أكْل مِش صِحّي بِتْحِبُّه؟

٨. تِعْرف أيْه عن أسْبانْيا؟

Expressions and Structures تعبيرات و تراكيب

Try to remember the Arabic expressions and structures from the article. Each English translation is followed by four choices, only one of which is correct. Refer back to the article to check your answers.

1. **as a group**

مجْموعةً — كمجْموعة

لِمجْموعة — زيّ مجْموعة

2. **every person**

الأشْخاص كُلُّه — كُلّ الشّخْص

الشّخْص كُلّ — كُلّ شخْص

3. **one and a half kilograms**

نُصّ كيلو — واحْدة و نُصّ كيلو

كيلو و نُصّ — واحِد نُصّ كيلو

4. **for the poorest people**

لِأفْقر شخْص — لِناس فقيرة

لِأفْقر ناس — لِلنّاس الفقيرة أوي

Answer Key and Translations

الإجابات والترجمات

Key Word Answers

challenge تحدّي • resident ساكِن • to lose weight خسّ • adminstration إدارة • at least على الأقلّ • goal هَدَف • charity جمْعية خَيْرية • to donate اِتْبرّع

Translation of the Article

1. **Spanish Town Wants to Lose 100,000 Kilos in Two Years**
2. There is a challenge in the Spanish municipality {town} of Narón that its residents lose 100,000 kilograms as a group within two years.
3. The translation of the name of the challenge in Spanish is "One Hundred Thousand Reasons for Weight."
4. The challenge started in January 2018, and after a year, people had [already] lost 46 kilos.
5. The population {number of residents} of Narón is 39,000 {person}.
6. This means that every person there should lose around 1.5 kilos in two years so that the town loses 100,000 kilos.
7. The administration of health {there} has said that there are 15,000 people who need to lose weight in the town.
8. The goal is that these people lose at least 10% of their weight.
9. There is a charity in the town that will donate food or milk to the poorest people in the town for each kilo people lose.

Phonemic Transcription of the Article

1. *madīna ʔasbaníyya 3áyza t(i)xíss(ə) mīt ʔalfə kīlu f(i) sanatēn*
2. *fī taɦáddi f(i) madīnit narōn ilʔasbaníyya ʔinnə sukkánha y(i)xíssu mīt ʔalfə kīlu ka-magmū3a f(i) sanatēn.*
3. *targámit ʔism ittaɦáddi bi-lʔasbāni híyya: mīt ʔalfə sábab li-lwázn.*
4. *ittaɦáddi bádaʔ fi yanāyir ʔalfēn wi tamantāšar, wi ba3də sána, innās kānu xássu sítta w(i) ʔarbi3īn ʔalf(ə) kīlu.*
5. *3ádad sukkān narōn tís3a w(i) talatīn ʔalfə šaxṣ;*
6. *yá3ni kullə šaxṣə h(i)nāk lāzim yixíssə ɦawāli kīlu w(i) nuṣṣ(ə) f(i) sanatēn 3ašān ilmadīna t(i)xíssə mīt ʔalfə kīlu.*

7. *ʔidārit iṣṣíḫḫa h(i)nāk ʔālit ʔinnə fī xamastāšar ʔalfə šaxṣ(ə) miḫtāg yixíss(ə) fi -lmadīna.*
8. *ilhádaf ʔinn innās dōl yixíssu 3ála -lʔaʔáll(ə) 3ášara fi -lmíyya min waznúhum.*
9. *fī gam3íyya xayríyya fi -lmadīna hatitbárra3 bi-ʔáklə ʔaw lában li-ʔáfʔar nās fi -lmadīna li-kúllə kīlu -nnās hayxissū.*

Translation of the Questions

1. What is the population of the city of Narón? 2. How many people need to lose weight? 3. What is the charity in the city going to do? 4. What is your opinion about this news? 5. Is weight a big problem in your town? 6. In your opinion, is exercise or eating healthy more important? Why? 7. What is the most unhealthy food that you love? 8. What do you know about Spain?

Answers to Expressions and Structures

1. as a group كمجْموعة
2. every person كُلّ شخْص
3. one and a half kilograms كيلو و نُصّ
4. for the poorest people لِأفْقر ناس

Notes

راجل و مراته من ليتوانيا كسبوا مسابقة "شيل زوجات"

فيه راجل و مراته من ليتوانيا كسبوا بطولة العالم لـ"شيل الزوجات" في فنلندا سنتين ورا بعض. الجايزة كانت وزن الست بيرة.

رجالة كتير و مراتاتهم من بلاد كتير بيشاركوا في المسابقة كل سنة في هلسينكي، عاصمة فنلندا.

عشان يكسبوا، الراجل كان لازم ينط و هو شايل مراته فوق حتت خشب كبير و يمشي في الماية في دقيقة و حوالي سبع ثواني بس.

قانون المسابقة بيقول إن الست لازم تكون أكبر من ١٧ سنة و وزنها يكون أكتر من ٤٩ كيلوجرام. الراجل و الست مش لازم يكونوا متجوزين بجد. يعني الرجالة اللي عايزين يشاركوا ممكن يروحوا مع أي ست.

مسابقات شيل الزوجات انتشرت بره فنلندا كمان. فيه دلوقتي مسابقات محلية بتتعمل في أستراليا و بولندا و إنجلترا و الولايات المتحدة.

Lithuanian Couple Wins Wife-Carrying Competition

Key Words — الكلمات

Study the key words and their definitions.

Translations	Definitions	Key Words
____________	أخد جايْزة	كِسِب (يِكْسَب)
____________	حاجة مُمْكِن تِكْسبْها	جايْزة (جَوايِز)
____________	مُنافْسة بيْن ناس كِتير عشان يِكْسبوا جايْزة	مُسابْقة
____________	تُقْل: وَزْني ٧٠ كيلو.	وَزْن (أَوْزان)
____________	إنّك تِرْفع حاجة مِن على الأرْض	شيْل
____________	ضرب الأرْض بِرِجْلُه عشان يِطْلع فوْق	نَطّ (يِنُطّ)
____________	قاعْدة	قانون (قَوانين)
____________	فِعْلاً	بِجَدّ
____________	بقى جُزْء مِن حاجة	شارِك (يِشارِك)
____________	جُوّه بلد؛ مِش عالمي	محلّي

Now match these translations to the key words above. Check your answers in the answer key.

carrying • competition • local • prize • really • rule •
to jump • to participate, take part • to win • weight

The Article المقالة

1 راجِل و مِراتُه مِن ليتْوانْيا كِسْبوا مُسابْقةْ "شيْل زَوْجات"

2 فيه راجِل و مِراتُه مِن ليتْوانْيا كِسْبوا بُطولةْ العالم لـ"شيْل الزَّوْجات" في فِنْلنْدا سنتيْن وَرا بعْض.

3 الجايْزة كانِت وَزْن السِّتّ بيرة.

4 رِجالة كِتير و مِراتاتْهُم مِن بِلاد كِتير بِيْشارْكوا في المُسابْقة كُلّ سنة في **هلْسينْكي**، عاصِمةْ فِنْلنْدا.

5 عشان يِكْسبوا، الرّاجِل كان لازِم يِنُطّ و هُوَّ شايِل مِراتُه فوْق حِتت خشب كبيرة و يِمْشي في المايّة في دِقيقة و حَوالي سبع ثَواني بسّ.

6 قانون المُسابْقة بِيْقول إنّ السِّتّ لازِم تِكون أكْبر مِن سبعْتاشر سنة و وَزْنها يِكون أكْتر مِن تِسْعة و أرْبِعين كيلوجْرام.

7 الرّاجِل و السِّتّ مِش لازِم يِكونوا مِتْجوِّزين بِجدّ.

8 يَعْني الرِّجالة اللي عايْزين يِشارْكوا مُمْكِن يِروحوا مع أيّ سِتّ.

9 مُسابقات شيْل الزَّوْجات اِنْتشرِت برّه فِنْلنْدا كمان.

10 فيه دِلْوَقْتي مُسابقات محلّيّة بِتِتْعمِل في أُسْترالْيا و بولنْدا و إنْجِلْتِـرا و الوِلايات المتّحِدة.

أسئلة الفهم Comprehension Questions

١. الرّاجِل و مِراتُه اللي كِسْبوا كانوا مِنينْ؟

٢. قانون المُسابْقة بِيْقول إنّ الرّاجِل و السِّتّ لازِم يِكونوا مِتْجوِّزين بِجدّ؟

٣. مُسابْقات شيْل الزَّوْجات بِتِتْعِمِل في فِنْلنْدا بسّ؟

أسئلة المناقشة Discussion Questions

٤. أيْه رأْيَك في المقالة دي؟

٥. مُمْكِن تِشارِك في المُسابْقة دي؟ ليْه؟

٦. بِتْحِبّ تِلْعب أَوْ تِتفرّج على أيّ رِياضة؟

٧. مين أشْهر لاعِب رِياضة في بلدك؟

٨. رُحْت فِنْلنْدا قبْل كِده؟ لَوْ آه، عملْت أيْه؟ لَوْ لأ، تِحِبّ تِروح؟

Expressions and Structures تعبيرات و تراكيب

Try to remember the Arabic expressions and structures from the article. Each English translation is followed by four choices, only one of which is correct. Refer back to the article to check your answers.

1. **two years in a row**

سنتينْ وَرا بعْض | سنتينْ بعْض وَرا
سنتينْ وَرا وَرا | سنة بعْض سنة

2. **they participate in the competition**

بِيْشارْكوا في المُسابْقة | بِيْشارْكوا على المُسابْقة
بِيْشارْكوا لِلمُسابْقة | بِيْشارْكوا المُسابْقة

3. **in order to win (so that they win)**

علشان بِيِكْسبوا | عشان يِكْسبوا
لِيَكْسبوا | في إنّ يِكْسبوا

4. **with any woman**

مع أنْهي سِتّ | مع أيّ سِتّ
مع كُلّ السِّتّات | مع كام سِتّ

Answer Key and Translations

الإجابات و الترجمات

Key Word Answers

to win كِسِب • prize جايْزة • competition مُسابْقة • weight وَزْن • carrying شيْل • to jump نَطّ • rule قانون • really بِجدّ • to participate, take part شارِك • local محلّي

Translation of the Article

1. **Lithuanian Couple Wins Wife-Carrying Competition**
2. {There is} a man and his wife from Lithuania [who] won the world championship of 'wife-carrying' in Finland two years in a row.
3. The prize was the weight of the woman in beer.
4. A lot of men and their wives from many countries participate in the competition every year in Helsinki, the Capital of Finland.
5. To win, the man had to jump while he was carrying his wife over large pieces of wood and walk in the water in a minute and about seven seconds.
6. The rule of the competition says that a woman has to be older than 17 years old and her weight more than 49 kilos.
7. A man and woman don't have to be actually married,
8. meaning the men who want to participate can go with any woman.
9. Wife-carrying competitions have spread outside Finland, as well.
10. There are now local competitions [that are] held {done} in Australia, Poland, England, and the US.

Phonemic Transcription of the Article

1. *rāgil wi mirātu min lituwánya kísbu musábʔit "šēl zawgāt"*
2. *fī rāgil wi mrātu min lituwánya kísbu buṭūlit il3ālam li-"šēl izzawgāt" fi finlánda sanatēn wára ba3ḍ.*
3. *ilgáyza kānit wazn issítt(ə) bīra.*
4. *rigāla kitīr wi mratáthum min bilād kitīr biyšárku fi -lmusábʔa kullə sána fi halsínki, 3aṣímit finlánda.*

5. *3ašān yiksábu, irrāgil kān lāzim yinútṭ, wi húwwa šāyil mirātu fōʔ ḫítat xášab kibīra w(i) yímši fi -lmáyya f(i) diʔīʔa wi ḫawāli sába3 sawāni bass.*
6. *qanūn ilmusábʔa biyʔūl ʔinn issíttə lāzim tikūn ʔákbar min saba3tāšar sána, wi waznáha y(i)kūn ʔáktar min tís3a w(i) ʔarbi3īn kilugrām.*
7. *irrāgil w issítt(ə) miš lāzim yikūnu mitgawwizīn bi-gádd.*
8. *yá3ni -rrigāla ílli 3ayzīn yišárku múmkin yirūḫu ma3 ʔayyə sitt.*
9. *musabaʔāt šēl izzawgāt intášarit bárra finlánda kamān.*
10. *fī dilwáʔti musabaʔāt maḫallíyya bitit3ímil fi ʔusturálya wi bulánda w ʔingiltíra w ilwilayāt ilmuttáḫida.*

Translation of the Questions

1. Where were the man and his wife who won from? 2. Does the competition's rule state that the man and woman must actually be married? 3. Do 'wife-carrying' competitions only take place in Finland? 4. What is your opinion of this article? 5. Could you take part in this competition? Why (not)? 6. Do you like to play or watch any sport? 7. Who is the most famous athlete in your country? 8. Have you been to Finland? If so, what did you do? If not, would you like to go?

Answers to Expressions and Structures

1. two years in a row سنتيْن وَرا بعْض
2. they participate in the competition بِيْشارْكوا في المُسابْقة
3. in order to win (so that they win) عشان يِكْسبوا
4. with any woman مع أيّ سِتّ

Notes

متحف فن تحت الماية فتح في أستراليا

المتحف الجديد الفن تحت الماية فتح في أستراليا في الحاجز المرجاني العظيم. المتحف على عمق ١٨ متر تحت الماية.

المتحف فيه تماثيل للفنان البريطاني چايسون ديكايرز تايلور اللي عمل أول جنينة تماثيل تحت الماية في جرينادا في ٢٠٠٦.

هدف المتحف الجديد إن الناس يهتموا بتغير المناخ و حماية الحواجز المرجانية. المتحف معمول من خامات بتساعد المرجان و كائنات بحرية تانية إنهم يكبروا.

وزن أكبر تمثال حوالي ٥٨ طن. جوه التمثال ده، فيه مكان ممكن تعيش فيه أسماك و كائنات بحرية تانية. فيه كمان فتحات عشان الغواصين يعوموا جوه التمثال.

المتحف هيخلق ١٨٢ فرصة عمل، و المفروض إنه يجيب ٥٠ خمسين ألف زائر لتاونزڤيل، المدينة اللي فيها المتحف، كل سنة. المتحف هيكون فيه تماثيل تانية في ٢٠٢١.

Museum of Underwater Art Opens in Australia

Key Words

الكلمات

Study the key words and their definitions.

Translations	Definitions	Key Words
________	هيْكل مِلوِّن بِيِتْكوِّن مِن حَيَوانات صُغيّرة في المايّة	حاجِز مُرْجاني (حَواجِز مُرْجانية)
________	المسافة مِن سطْح حاجة لِقاعْها	عُمْق (أعْماق)
________	نحْت: تمْثال الحُرّية في نْيويوْرْك.	تِمْثال (تماثيل)
________	شخْص بِيِعْمِل فنّ، زيّ الرّسْم أَوْ الغُنا، إلخ.	فنّان / فنّانة
________	بِيْحِبّ و عايِز يِعْرف أكْتر عن حاجة	اِهْتمّ (يِهْتمّ) بِـ
________	اِخْتِلاف درجِةْ الحرارة، بِسبب الاِحْتِباس الحراري مثلاً	تغيُّر المُناخ
________	الحِفاظ على	حِمايَة
________	مادّة، زيّ الخشب، الحديد، القُطْن، البِلاسْتِك، إلخ.	خامة
________	بقى أكْبر	كِبِر (يِكْبر)
________	حاجة بِتْعيش؛ فيها حَياة	كائِن
________	فتح شُغْل	خلق فُرْصِةْ عمل (فُرَص عمَل)

Now match these translations to the key words above. Check your answers in the answer key.

artist • climate change • coral reef • creature • depth • protection • raw material • sculpture • to become bigger; grow • to care about; take an interest in • to create a job opportunity

The Article

المقالة

1 متْحف فنّ تحْت المايّة فتح في أُسْتُرالْيا

2 المتْحف الجِديد "الفنّ تحْت المايّة" فتح في أُسْتُرالْيا في الحاجِز المُرْجاني العظيم.

3 المتْحف على عُمْق تمانْتاشر مِتْر تحْت المايّة.

4 المتْحف فيه تماثيل لِلفنّان البريطاني **چايْسون ديكايرْز تايْلور** اللي عمل أوّل جِنيْنة تماثيل تحْت المايّة في جِرينادا في ألْفيْن و سِتّة.

5 هدف المتْحف الجِديد إنّ النّاس يِهْتمّوا بِتغيرّ المُناخ و حِمايةْ الحواجِز المُرْجانية.

6 المتْحف معْمول مِن خامات بِتْساعِد المُرْجان و كائِنات بحْرية تانْيَة إنُّهُم يِكْبروا.

7 وَزْن أكْبر تِمْثال حَوالي تمانْيَة و خمْسين طِنّ.

8 جُوّه التِّمْثال ده، فيه مكان مُمْكِن تِعيش فيه أسْماك و كائنات بحْرية تانْيَة.

9 فيه كمان فتحات عشان الغوّاصين يِعوموا جُوّه التِّمْثال.

10 المتْحف هَيخْلق مية اِتْنيْن و تمانين فُرْصِةْ عمل، و المفْروض إنُّه يِجيب خمْسين ألْف زائِر **لِتاوْنزْفيل**، المدينة اللي فيها المتْحف، كُلّ سنة.

11 المتْحف هَيكون فيه تماثيل تانْيَة في ألْفيْن واحِد و عِشْرين.

Comprehension Questions أسئلة الفهم

١. أيْه إسْم المدينة اللي فيها المتْحف؟

٢. مين عمل أوِّل جِنيْنةْ تماثيل تحْت المايّة؟

٣. أيْه هدف المتْحف ده؟

Discussion Questions أسئلة المناقشة

٤. أيْه رأْيَك في المتْحف ده؟

٥. بتِعْرف تِعوم أَوْ تِغْطس؟ لَوْ آه، اتْعلِّمْت إمْتى و ليْه؟

٦. عُمْرك ربّيْت سمك أَوْ أيّ حَيَوانات أليفة؟

٧. تِعْرف أيْه عن أُسْترُالْيا؟

٨. شُفْت مرْجان قبْل كِده؟ لَوْ آه، فيْن؟ لَوْ لأ، تِحِبّ تِشوف؟

Expressions and Structures تعبيرات و تراكيب

Try to remember the Arabic expressions and structures from the article. Each English translation is followed by four choices, only one of which is correct. Refer back to the article to check your answers.

1. **(at a depth of) 18m underwater**

تحْت المايّة في العُمْق مِن ١٨ مِترْ
عميق ١٨ مِترْ تحْت المايّة
١٨ مِترْ عميق تحْت المايّة
على عُمْق ١٨ مِترْ تحْت المايّة

2. **in 2006**

في عِشْرين و سِتّة
في ألْفينْ سِتّة
في اِتْنينْ صِفْر صِفْر سِتّة
في ألْفينْ و سِتّة

3. **the museum is made of...**

المتْحف المعْمول مِن
المتْحف معْمول مِن
المتْحف عُمِلَ مِن
المتْحف بيِتْعِمِل مِن

4. **there will be**

هِناك بيْكون
كائِن
هَيْكون فيه
كان فيه

Answer Key and Translations

الإجابات و الترجمات

Key Word Answers

coral reef حاجِز مُرْجاني • depth عُمق • sculpture تِمْثال • artist فنّان • to care about; take an interest in اِهْتمّ بـ • climate change تغيُّر المناخ • protection حِماية • raw material خامة • to become bigger; grow كِبِر • creature كائِن • to create a job opportunity خلق فُرْصِة عمل

Translation of the Article

1. **Museum of Underwater Art Opens in Australia**
2. The new Museum of Underwater Art opened in Australia in the Great Barrier Reef.
3. The museum is 18 meters underwater.
4. There are sculptures in the museum from the British artist Jason deCaires Taylor, who made the first park of underwater sculptures in Grenada in 2006.
5. The goal of the new museum is that people become interested in climate change and the protection of coral reefs.
6. The museum is made of materials that help the coral and other sea animals grow.
7. The weight of the biggest sculpture is about 58 tons.
8. Inside this sculpture, there is a place in which fish and other sea animals can live.
9. There are also openings to allow divers to swim inside of the sculpture.
10. The museum will create 182 job opportunities, and it is supposed to bring fifty thousand visitors to Townsville, the city where the museum is located, every year.
11. There will be other sculptures in the museum in 2021.

Phonemic Transcription of the Article

1. *máthaf fannə taht ilmáyya fátah fi ʔusturálya*
2. *ilmáthaf ilgidīd "ilfánnə taht ilmáyya" fátah fi ʔusturálya fi -lhāgiz ilmurgāni -l3azīm.*

3. *ilmátḫaf 3ála 3úmq(ə) tamantāšar mitr(ə) taḫt ilmáyya.*
4. *ilmátḫaf fī tamasīl li-lfannān ilbiriṭāni [Jason deCaires Taylor] ílli 3ámal ʔáwwil ginēnit tamasīl taḫt ilmáyya fi grināda fi ʔalfēn wi sítta.*
5. *hádaf ilmátḫaf ilgidīd ʔinn innās yihtámmu b(i)-taɣáyyur ilmunāx wi ḫimāyit ilḫawāgiz ilmurganíyya.*
6. *ilmátḫaf ma3mūl min xamāt bitsā3id ilmurgān wi kaʔināt baḫríyya tánya ʔinnúhum yikbáru.*
7. *waznə ʔákbar timsāl ḫawāli tamánya wi xamsīn ṭinn.*
8. *gúwwa -ttimsāl da, fī makān múmkin ti3īš fī ʔasmāk wi kaʔināt baḫríyya tánya.*
9. *fī kamān fataḫāt 3ašān ilɣawwaṣīn yi3ūmu gúwwa -ttimsāl.*
10. *ilmátḫaf hayíxlaʔ míyya -tnēn wi tamanīn fúrṣit 3ámal, w ilmafrūḍ ʔínnu y(i)gīb xamsīn ʔalfə zāʔir li-[Townsville], ilmadīna (i)lli fīha -lmátḫaf, kullə sána.*
11. *ilmátḫaf haykūn fī tamasīl tánya fi ʔalfēn wāḫid wi 3išrīn.*

Translation of the Questions

1. What is the name of the town where the museum is? 2. Who made the first park of underwater sculptures? 3. What is the goal of the museum? 4. What is your opinion of the museum? 5. Do you know how to swim or dive? If so, when did you learn and why? 6. Have you ever had fish or [other] pets? 7. What do you know about Australia? 8. Have you seen coral before? If so, where? If not, would you like to?

Answers to Expressions and Structures

1. (at a depth of) 18m underwater على عُمْق ١٨ مِتْر تَحْت المايّة
2. in 2006 في ألْفين و سِتّة
3. the museum is made of... المتْحف معْمول مِن
4. there will be هَيْكون فيه

Notes

أطفال أونتاريو هيتعلموا البرمجة و الإدارة المالية من سن ست سنين

رئيس وزرة أونتاريو دوج فورد قال إن منهج الحساب الجديد في أونتاريو، كندا، هيكون فيه دروس في البرمجة و الإدارة المالية الشخصية للتلاميذ من سن ٦ سنين لسن ١٤ سنة.

آخر مرة منهج الحساب اتغير في أونتاريو كان في ٢٠٠٥. وزير التعليم ستيڤن ليتشي بيقول إن من ساعتها، فيه تلاميذ كتير أوي مبيتعلموش المهارات اللي هما محتاجينها عشان ياخدوا قرارات ليها علاقة بالحساب و الإدارة المالية.

فورد بيقول إن البرمجة و الإدارة المالية هيساعدوا الأطفال يلاقوا شغل و يبقوا ناجحين. هو بيقول برضه إن فيه حاجات كتير اتغيرت من ٢٠٠٥ و عشان كده، التعليم محتاج يتغير هو كمان.

٩ Ontario Kids to Learn Coding and Finance From Age Six

Key Words — الكلمات

Study the key words and their definitions.

Translations	Definitions	Key Words
____________	رئيس حُكومة: **چاسْتن تْرودو** رئيس وُزرة كندا	رئيس وُزرا
____________	مجْموعِة دُروس لِلْمُذاكرة	منْهج (مناهِج)
____________	عمل برامج كُمْپْيوتر	برْمجة
____________	تنْظيم الشّخْص لِفْلوسُه	الإدارة المالية الشخْصية
____________	طالِب، غالِباً بِيْكون طِفْل	تِلْميذ / تِلْميذة (تلاميذ)
____________	مِن الوَقْت ده	مِن ساعِتْها
____________	القُدْرة على عمل حاجة كُوَيِّس	مهارة
____________	تَصَرُّف	قرار
____________	مُرْتبِط بـ	ليه علاقة بـ
____________	أُسْلوب دِراسة	تعْليم

Now match these translations to the key words above. Check your answers in the answer key.

curriculum • decision • education • personal finance • prime minister • programming • pupil, student • related to • since then • skill

The Article

المقالة

1 أطْفال **أونْتارْيو** هَيِتْعلِّموا البرْمجة و الإدارة المالية مِن سِنّ سِتّ سِنين

2 رئيس وُزرِةْ **أونْتارْيو دوج فورْد** قال إنّ منْهج الحِساب الجِديد في **أونْتارْيو**، كندا، هَيْكون فيه دُروس في البرْمجة و الإدارة المالية الشخْصية لِلتّلاميذ مِن سِنّ سِتّ سِنين لِسِنّ أرْبعْتاشر سنة.

3 آخِر مرّة منْهج الحِساب اِتْغيرّ في **أونْتارْيو** كان في ألْفينْ و خمْسة.

4 وَزير التّعْليم **سْتيڤن ليتْشي** بِيْقول إنّ مِن ساعِتْها، فيه تلاميذ كِتير أوي مبيِتْعلِّموش المهارات اللي هُمّا مِحْتاجينْها عشان ياخْدوا قرّارات ليها عِلاقة بِالحِساب و الإدارة المالية.

5 **فورْد** بِيْقول إنّ البرْمجة و الإدارة المالية هَيْساعْدوا الأطْفال يِلاقوا شُغْل و يِبْقوا ناجْحين.

6 هُوَّ بِيْقول برْضُه إنّ فيه حاجات كِتير اِتْغيرّت مِن ألْفينْ و خمْسة و عشان كِده، التّعْليم مِحْتاج يِتْغيرّ هُوَّ كمان.

أسئلة الفهم Comprehension Questions

١. أطْفال **أونْتارْيو** هَيتْعلِّموا أيْه؟

٢. إمْتى آخِر مرّة منْهج الحِساب في **أونْتارْيو** اِتْغيرّ؟

٣. مين وَزير التّعْليم في **أونْتارْيو**؟

أسئلة المناقشة Discussion Questions

٤. أيْه رأْيَك في فِكْرِةْ المنْهج الجِديد؟

٥. كُنْت شاطِر في الحِساب لمّا كُنْت في المدْرسة؟ أيْه المَوادّ اللي كُنْت بِتْحِبْها؟

٦. بتِعْرف برْمجة؟ لَوْ آه، اِتْعلِّمْت إزّاي؟ لَوْ لأ، تِحِبّ تِتْعلِّم؟

٧. لَوْ كُنْت وَزير التّعْليم في بلدك، هتْغيرّ أيْه؟

٨. تِفْتِكِر كُلّ الأطْفال لازِم يِتْعلِّموا برْمجة؟

Expressions and Structures تعبيرات و تراكيب

Try to remember the Arabic expressions and structures from the article. Each English translation is followed by four choices, only one of which is correct. Refer back to the article to check your answers.

1. **from the age of six**

   مِن ستّة سِنين

   مِن سِنّ ستّ سنة

   مِن سِنّ ستّ سِنين

   سِنّ مِن ستّة

2. **since then**

   مِن ساعِتْها

   مِن الوَقْت

   مِن بعْديْن

   مِن ساعة دي

3. **so many students**

   تلاميذ أوي كِتير

   أوي كِتير تلاميذ

   كِتير أوي تلاميذ

   تلاميذ كِتير أوي

4. **related to**

   عنْدُه عِلاقة لـِ

   معْلوقة بـِ

   اللي العِلاقة مِن

   ليها عِلاقة بـِ

Answer Key and Translations

الإجابات و الترجمات

Key Word Answers

prime minister رئيس وُزرا • curriculum منْهج • programming برْمجة • personal finance الإدارة المالية الشخْصية • pupil, student تِلْميذ • since then من ساعتْها • skill مهارة • decision قرار • related to ليه علاقة بـ • education تعْليم

Translation of the Article

1. **Ontario Kids to Learn Coding and Finance From Age Six**
2. The premier {president of prime ministers} of Ontario, Doug Ford, said that the new math curriculum in Ontario, Canada, will include classes in programming and personal finance for pupils from the age of six to {the age of} fourteen.
3. The last time the math curriculum was changed in Ontario was in 2005.
4. The minister of education, Stephen Lecce, says that since that time, there have been so many students not learning the skills that they need to make decisions related to math and personal finance.
5. Ford says that programming and personal finance will help kids find jobs and be successful.
6. He also says that {there are} many things [that] have changed since 2005, and therefore, education needs to change, as well.

Phonemic Transcription of the Article

1. *ʔaṭfāl ʔuntáryu hayit3allímu -lbarmága w ilʔidāra -lmalíyya min sinn(ə) sittə s(i)nīn*
2. *raʔīs wúzarit ʔuntáryu [Doug Ford] ʔāl ʔinnə mánhag ilḥisāb ilgidīd fi ʔuntáryu, kánada, haykūn fī durūs fi -lbarmága w ilʔidāra -lmalíyya ilšaxṣíyya li-ttalamīz min sinnə sittə s(i)nīn li-sinn(ə) ʔarba3tāšar sána.*
3. *āxir márra mánhag ilḥisāb itɣáyyar fi ʔuntáryu kān fi ʔalfēn wi xámsa.*
4. *wazīr itta3līm, [Stephen Lecce], biyʔūl ʔinnə min sa3ítha, fī talamīz kitīr ʔáwi ma-byit3allimūš ilmaharāt ílli húmma miḥtagínha 3ašān yáxdu qarrarāt līha 3ilāqa bi-lḥisāb w ilʔidāra -lmalíyya.*

5. *[Ford] biyʔūl ʔinn ilbarmága w ilʔidāra -lmalíyya haysá3du -lʔaṭfāl yilāʔu šuɣl, wi yíbʔu nagḫīn.*
6. *húwwa biyʔūl bárḍu ʔinnə fī ḫagāt kitīr ityayyárit min ʔalfēn wi xámsa wi 3ašān kída, itta3līm miḫtāg yitiɣáyyar húwwa kamān.*

Translation of the Questions

1. What will children in Ontario be learning? 2. When was the last time that Ontario's math curriculum changed? 3. Who is the minister of eduation in Ontario? 4. What is your opinion on the idea behind the new curriculum? 5. Were you good at math when you were in school? What subjects did you like? 6. Do you know programming? If so, how did you learn it? If not, would you like to? 7. If you were the minister/secretary of education in your country, what would you change? 8. Do you think all children need to learn programming?

Answers to Expressions and Structures

1. from the age of six مِن سِنّ سِتّ سِنين
2. since then مِن ساعِتْها
3. so many students تلاميذ كِتير أوي
4. related to ليها عِلاقة بِـ

Notes

مصر فتحت الهرم المنحني للزوار

في يوم ١٣ يوليه ٢٠١٩، مصر فتحت هرمين للزوار لأول مرة من ١٩٦٥.

وزير الآثارالمصري قال إن الزوار ممكن دلوقتي يزوروا الهرم المنحني و هرم تاني صغير جنبه في دهشور جنوب القاهرة.

الهرم المنحني اتبنى حوالي سنة ٢٦٠٠ ق.م للملك سنفرو. شكل الهرم مختلف عن بقية الأهرامات اللي اتبنت بعد كده. الشكل مختلف بسبب مشاكل ظهرت بعد ما اتبنى.

ناس أقل بقوا بيزوروا مصر من ساعة ما حكومة حسني مبارك وقعت في ٢٠١١. و الحكومة بتاعة دلوقتي شغالة جامد عشان الزوار يزيدوا.

المتحف المصري الكبير المفروض يفتح في ٢٠٢١، و هيكون فيه ٥٠ ألف قطعة أثرية فرعونية. المتحف أخد ١٠ سنين عشان يتبني، و اتكلف أكتر من مليار دولار أمريكي.

١٠ Egypt Opens Bent Pyramid to Visitors

Key Words الكلمات

Study the key words and their definitions.

Translations	Definitions	Key Words
________	مبْنى على شكْل مُثلّث	هرم (أهْرامات)
________	حدّ بيْزور شخْص أَوْ مكان	زائِر / زائِرة (زُوّار)
________	رئيس قِسم أساسي في الحُكومة	وَزير / وَزيرة (وُزرا)
________	حاجة قديمة جِدّاً و غالْية جِدّاً	أثر (آثار)
________	المبْني لِلمجْهول مِن "بنى"	اِتْبنى (يِتْبِني)
________	اللي فاضِل	بقية
________	بان	ظهر (يِظْهر)
________	بقى أكْتر	زاد (يِزيد)
________	حِتّة	قِطْعَة (قِطَع)
________	قديم جِدّاً و غالي جِدّاً	أثري
________	اِحْتاج فِلوس	اِتْكلِّف (يِتْكلِّف)

Now match these translations to the key words above. Check your answers in the answer key.

ancient • artifact • minister • piece • pyramid • the rest • to appear; to arise • to be built • to cost • to increase • visitor

The Article المقالة

1 مصْر فتحِت الهرم المنْحني للِزُّوّار

2 في يوْم تلاتّاشر يوليْه ألْفينْ و تِسعْتاشر، مصْر فتحِت هرمينْ للِزُّوّار لأِوِّل مرّة مِن ألْف تُسْعُمية خمْسة و ستّين.

3 وَزير الآثارالمصْري قال إنّ الزُّوّار مُمْكِن دِلْوَقْتي يِزوروا الهرم المنْحني و هرم تاني صُغيرّ جنْبُه في دهْشور جُنوب القاهِرة.

4 الهرم المنْحني اِتْبنى حَوالي سنةْ ألْفينْ و سُتُّمية قبْل الميلاد للِملك سِنِفْرو.

5 شكْل الهرم مُخْتلِف عن بقيةْ الأهْرامات اللي اِتْبنِت بعْد كِده.

6 الشّكْل مُخْتلِف بِسبب مشاكِل ظهرِت بعْد ما اتْبنى.

7 ناس أقلّ بقوا بِيْزوروا مصْر مِن ساعِةْ ما حُكومِةْ حُسْني مُبارك وِقْعِت في ألْفينْ و حِداشر.

8 و الحُكومة بِتاعِةْ دِلْوَقْتي شغّالة جامِد عشان الزُّوّار يِزيدوا.

9 المتْحف المصْري الكِبير المفْروض يِفْتح في ألْفينْ واحِد و عِشْرين، و هَيْكون فيه خمْسين ألْف قِطْعة أثرية فرْعونية.

10 المتْحف أخد عشر سِنين عشان يِتْبِني، و اِتْكلِّف أكْتر مِن مِلْيار دولار أمْريكي.

أسئلة الفهم Comprehension Questions

١. مصْر فتحِت كام هرم؟

٢. الهرم المُنْحني اِتْبنى لِمين؟

٣. المتْحف المصْري الكِبير اِتْكلِّف كام؟

أسئلة المناقشة Discussion Questions

٤. أيْه رأْيَك في فتْح الهرمينْ دوْل لِلزُّوّار؟

٥. زُرْت أيّ مكان أثري في مصْر قبْل كِده؟

٦. بِتْحِبّ زِيارةْ المتاحِف؟ ليْه؟

٧. لَوْ قدِرْت تِعيش في أيّ فتْرة في التّاريخ، هتِخْتار أنْهي فتْرة؟ ليْه؟

٨. كُنْت بِتْحِبّ التّاريخ في المدْرسة؟

Expressions and Structures تعبيرات و تراكيب

Try to remember the Arabic expressions and structures from the article. Each English translation is followed by four choices, only one of which is correct. Refer back to the article to check your answers.

1. **for the first time**

    - لِأوِّل مرّة
    - مرّة الأولى
    - الأوِّل
    - لِأوِّل وَقْت

2. **since...**

    - مِن ساعْتينْ
    - مِن ساعةْ ما
    - مِن السّاعة إنّ
    - مِن ساعِتْها ما

3. **the current government**

    - الحُكومة الوَقْتية دي
    - حُكومة بِتاعِةْ دِلْوَقْتي
    - دِلْوَقْتي بِتاع الحُكومة
    - الحُكومة بِتاعِةْ دِلْوَقْتي

4. **the museum took ten years to build**

    - المتْحف اِتْبنى بعْد عشر سِنين
    - المتْحف أخد عشر سِنين عشان يِتْبِني
    - المتْحف كان لازِم يِتْبِني في عشر سِنين
    - المتْحف اِتْكلِّف عشر سِنين عشان اِتْبنى

Answer Key and Translations الإجابات و الترجمات

Key Word Answers

pyramid هرم • visitor زائِر • minister وَزير • artifact أثر • to be built اِتْبنى • the rest بقية • to appear; to arise ظهر • to increase زاد • piece قِطْعَة • ancient أثري • to cost اِتْكلِّف

Translation of the Article

1. **Egypt Opens Bent Pyramid to Visitors**
2. On {day} 13 July 2019, Egypt opened two pyramids to tourists for the first time since 1965.
3. The Egyptian Minister of Antiquities said that visitors can now visit the Bent Pyramid and another small pyramid next to it in Dahshour, south of Cairo.
4. The Bent Pyramid was built around the year 2600 BC {before the birth} for King Sneferu.
5. The shape of the pyramid is different from the rest of the pyramids that were built after that.
6. The shape is different due to problems that arose after it was built.
7. Fewer people have been {became} visiting Egypt since the government of Hosni Mubarak fell in 2011.
8. The current government is working hard so that the [number of] visitors increase.
9. The Grand Egyptian Museum is supposed to open in 2021 and will have 50,000 ancient pharaonic artifacts.
10. The museum took ten years to build and cost more than a billion US dollars.

Phonemic Transcription of the Article

1. *maṣr(ə) fátaḫit ilháram ilmunḫáni li-zzuwwār*
2. *fi yōm talattāšar yúlya ʔalfēn wi tisa3tāšar, maṣrə fátaḫit haramēn li-zzuwwār li-ʔáwwil márra min ʔalf(ə) tus3umíyya xámsa wi sittīn.*
3. *wazīr ilʔasār ilmáṣri ʔāl ʔinn izzuwwār múmkin dilwáʔti yizūru -lháram ilmunḫáni wi háram tāni ṣ(u)ɣáyyar gánbu f(i) dahšūr gunūb ilqāhíra.*
4. *ilháram ilmunḫáni (i)tbána ḫawāli sánat ʔalfēn wi suttumíyya ʔabl ilmilād li-lmálik sinífru.*

5. *šakl ilháram muxtálif 3an baʔíyyit ilʔahramāt ílli -tbánit ba3də kída.*
6. *iššáklə muxtálif bi-sábab mašākil ẓáharit ba3də ma -tbána.*
7. *nās ʔaʔáll(ə) báʔu biyzūru maṣr(ə) min sā3it ma ɧ(u)kūmit ɧúsni mubārak wíʔ3it fi ʔalfēn wi ɧidāšar.*
8. *w ilɧukūma bitā3it dilwáʔti šaɣɣāla gāmid 3ašān izzuwwār yizīdu.*
9. *ilmátɧaf ilmáṣri -lkibīr ilmafrūḍ yíftaɧ fi ʔalfēn wāɧid wi 3išrīn, wi haykūn fī xamsīn ʔalfə qíṭ3a ʔasaríyya far3uníyya.*
10. *ilmátɧaf ʔáxad 3ášar sinīn 3ašān yitbíni, w itkállif ʔáktar min milyār dulār ʔamrīki.*

Translation of the Questions

1. How many pyramids did Egypt open? 2. Who was the Bent Pyramid built for? 3. How much did the Grand Egyptian Museum (GEM) cost? 4. What is your opinion on opening these two pyramids to visitors? 5. Have you visited any ancient site in Egypt? 6. Do you like visiting museums? Why (not)? 7. If you could live in any period in history, which period would you choose? And why? 8. Did you like history in school?

Answers to Expressions and Structures

1. for the first time لِأوِّل مرّة
2. since... مِن ساعةْ ما
3. the current government الحْكومة بِتاعةْ دِلْوَقْتي
4. the museum took ten years to build المتْحف أخد عشر سِنين عشان يِتْبِني

Notes

معظم الأمريكان عايزين يشتغلوا من البيت

فيه إحصائية من شركة آي بي إم اتعملت في إبريل ٢٠٢٠ لقت إن ٥٤٪ في المية من البالغين بيفضلوا يشتغلوا من البيت بعد ما وباء كورونا ينتهي.

الإحصائية اللي اتعملت على ٢٥ ألف شخص بالغ أمريكي لقت إن أكتر من نصهم كانوا عايزين يشتغلوا من البيت معظم الوقت، و ٧٥٪ منهم فضلوا إن يبقى عندهم خيار إنهم يشتغلوا من البيت من وقت للتاني.

الإحصائية برضه سألت الناس عن رأيهم في المواصلات و لقت إنه اتغير.

أكتر من ٢٠٪ قالوا إنهم مش هيستعملوا المواصلات العامة، و ٢٨٪ قالوا إنهم هيستخدموها أقل. أكتر من نص البالغين قالوا إنهم هيستعملوا أوبر و ليفت أقل من الأول أو مش هيستعملوهم خالص.

Most Americans Want to Work From Home

Key Words

الكلمات

Study the key words and their definitions.

Translations	Definitions	Key Words
____________	دِراسة بِتِسْأل أسْئِلة لِعدد مِن النّاس	إحْصائية
____________	المبْني لِلمجْهول مِن "عمل"	اِتْعمل (يِتْعِمِل)
____________	شخْص كبِير؛ مِش طِفْل	بالغ / بالْغة
____________	حبّ حاجة أكْتر	فضّل (يِفضّل)
____________	حاجة مُمْكِن تِخْتارْها	خِيار
____________	خِلِص	اِنْتهى (يِنْتِهي)
____________	نِظام أوتوبيسات، قُطْرة، إلخ. لِكُلّ النّاس	مُواصْلات عامّة
____________	بقى مُخْتلِف	اِتْغيرّ (يِتْغيرّ)
____________	اِسْتخْدِم	اِسْتعْمِل (يِسْتعْمِل)

Now match these translations to the key words above. Check your answers in the answer key.

adult • option • public transportation • survey • to be made • to change • to end • to prefer • to use

The Article المقالة

1 مُعْظم الأمْريكان عايْزين يِشْتغلوا مِن البيْت

2 فيه إحْصائية مِن شرْكِةْ **آي بي إم** اِتْعملِت في إبْريل عِشْرين عِشْرين لقِت
إنّ أرْبعة و خمْسين في المية مِن البالْغين بِيْفضّلوا يِشْتغلوا مِن البيْت
بعْد ما وَباء كوروْنا يِنْتِهي.

3 الإحْصائية اللي اِتْعملِت على خمْسة و عِشْرين ألْف شخْص بالغ أمْريكي
لقِت إنّ أكْتر مِن نُصُّهْم كانوا عايْزين يِشْتغلوا مِن البيْت مُعْظم الوَقْت،

4 و خمْسة و سبْعين في المية مِنْهُم فضّلوا إنّ يِبْقى عنْدُهْم خِيار إنُّهُمْ
يِشْتغلوا مِن البيْت مِن وَقْت لِلتّاني.

5 الإحْصائية برْضُه سألِت النّاس عن رأْيُهْم في المُواصْلات و لقِت إنُّه
اتْغيرّ.

6 أكْتر مِن عِشْرين في المية قالوا إنُّهُمْ مِش هَيِسْتعْمِلوا المُواصْلات
العامّة،

7 و تمانْيَة و عِشْرين في المية قالوا إنُّهُمْ هَيِسْتخْدموها أقلّ.

8 أكْتر مِن نُصّ البالْغين قالوا إنُّهُمْ هَيِسْتعْمِلوا **أوبر** و **ليفْت** أقلّ مِن الأوِّل
أوْ مِش هَيِسْتعْملوهُمْ خالِص.

أسئلة الفهم Comprehension Questions

١. أكْتر مِن نُصّ الأمْريكان مِش عايْزين يِشْتغلوا مِن البيْت. صحّ وَلّا غلط؟

٢. الإحْصائية اِتْعملِت على كام شخْص؟

٣. رأْي النّاس في المُواصْلات اِتْغيرّ؟

أسئلة المناقشة Discussion Questions

٤. أنْهي أحْسن بِالنِّسْبة لك، الشُّغْل في البيْت وَلّا برّه البيْت؟ ليْه؟

٥. فيه مُشْكِلة مُواصْلات في بلدك؟ لَوْ آه، تِفْتِكِر أيْه الحلّ؟

٦. لَوْ إنْتَ مُدير شِرْكة، هتْخلّي المُوَظّفين يِشْتغلوا مِن البيْت؟ ليْه؟

٧. بِتْحِبّ أيْه و مبِتْحِبِّش أيْه في شُغْلك؟

٨. لَوْ هتِخْتار تِشْتغل أيّ شُغْل تاني غيْر شُغْلك، هتِشْتغل أيْه؟

Expressions and Structures تعبيرات و تراكيب

Try to remember the Arabic expressions and structures from the article. Each English translation is followed by four choices, only one of which is correct. Refer back to the article to check your answers.

1. **a survey was made**

فيه إحْصائية كانِت معْمول

فيه إحْصائية اِتْعملِت

فيه إحْصائية عملِتْها

فيه إحْصائية اِتْعلِّمِت

2. **most of the time**

أعْظم الوَقْت

الوَقْت المُعْظم

مُعْظم مِن الوَقْت

مُعْظم الوَقْت

3. **asked people about**

سألِت لِلنّاس عن

سألِت عن النّاس إنّ

سألِت النّاس عن

سألِت النّاس في

4. **not... at all**

مِش... خالِص

مِش... خلاص

مِش... في الكُلّ

مِش... على الأقلّ

Answer Key and Translations

الإجابات و الترجمات

Key Word Answers

survey إحْصائية • to be made اِتْعمل • adult بالغ • to prefer فضّل • option خِيار • to end اِنْتهى • public transportation مُواصْلات عامّة • to change اِتْغيّر • to use اِسْتعْمِل

Translation of the Article

1. **Most Americans Want to Work From Home**
2. {There is} a survey from {the company} IBM [that was] made in April 2020 found that 54% of adults prefer to work from home after the coronavirus pandemic ends.
3. The survey, which was made on 25,000 American adults, found that more than half of them want to work from home most of the time,
4. and 75% of them preferred to have the option to work from home from time to time.
5. The survey also asked people about their opinion on transportation and found that it had changed.
6. More than 20% said they would not use public transportation,
7. and 28% said they would use it less often.
8. More than half of adults said that they would use Uber and Lyft less than before or would not use them at all.

Phonemic Transcription of the Article

1. *mú3ẓam ilʔamrikān 3ayzīn yištáɣalu min ilbēt*
2. *fī ʔiḫṣaʔíyya min šírkit [IBM] it3ámalit fi ʔibrīl 3išrīn 3išrīn láʔit ʔinnə ʔarbá3a wi xamsīn fi -lmíyya min ilbalɣīn biyfaḍḍálu yištáɣalu min ilbēt ba3də ma wabāʔ kurōna yintíhi.*
3. *ilʔiḫṣaʔíyya (í)lli -t3ámalit 3ála xámsa w 3išrīn ʔalfə šaxṣə bāliɣ ʔamrīki láʔit ʔinnə ʔáktar min nuṣṣúhum kānu 3ayzīn yištáɣalu min ilbēt mú3ẓam ilwáʔt,*
4. *wi xámsa wi sab3īn fi -lmíyya mínhum faḍḍálu ʔinnə yíbʔa 3andúhum xiyār ʔinnúhum yištáɣalu min ilbēt min waʔtə li-ttāni.*
5. *ilʔiḫṣaʔíyya bárḍu sáʔalit innās 3an raʔyúhum fi -lmuwaṣlāt wi láʔit ʔínnu -tɣáyyar.*

6. *ʔáktar min 3išrīn fi -lmíyya ʔālu ʔinnúhum miš hayista3mílu (i)lmuwaṣlāt il3ámma,*
7. *wi tamánya wi 3išrīn fi -lmíyya ʔālu ʔinnúhum hayistaxdimūha ʔaʔáll.*
8. *ʔáktar min nuṣṣ ilbalyīn ʔālu ʔinnúhum hayista3mílu [Uber] wi [Lyft] ʔaʔáll(ə) min ilʔáwwil ʔaw miš hayista3milūhum xāliṣ.*

Translation of the Questions

1. More than half of Americans don't want to work from home. True or false? 2. How many people was the survey made on? 3. Has people's opinion of public transportation changed? 4. Which is better for you, working at home or outside the home? Why? 5. Are there transportation problems in your country? If so, what do you think is the solution? 6. If you were the manager of a company, would you let employees work from home? Why (not)? 7. What do you like and not like about your job? 8. If you were to choose to have any other job [than the one you have], what would you do?

Answers to Expressions and Structures

1. a survey was made فيه إحْصائية اِتْعملت
2. most of the time مُعْظم الوَقْت
3. asked people about سألِت النّاس عن
4. not... at all مِش... خالِص

Notes

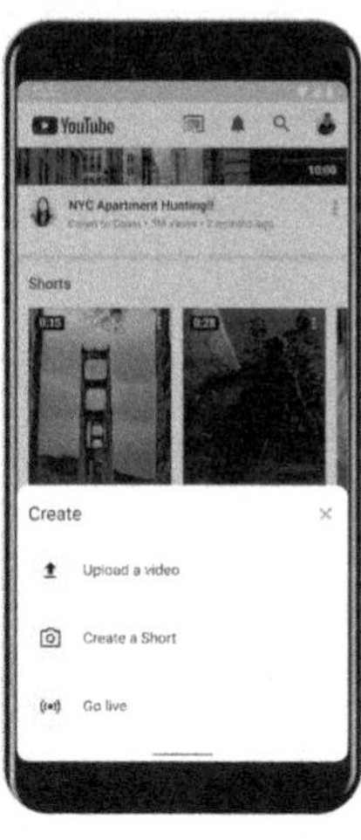

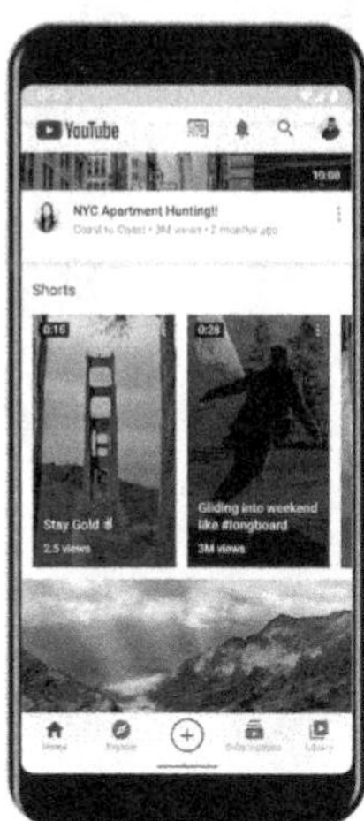

خاصية شورتس على يوتيوب هتنافس تيك توك

فيه أخبار إن يوتيوب دلوقتي شغال على خاصية جديدة إسمها شورتش عشان ينافس بيها تيك توك.

الناس ممكن يعملوا على تيك توك ڤيديوهات ١٥ ثانية. ٨٠٪ من اللي بيستعملوا تيك توك في الولايات المتحدة أعمارهم ١٦-٣٤ سنة.

تيك توك بدأ في الصين في ٢٠١٦، و أكتر من مليار شخص بيستعملوه كل شهر. بس فيه ٢ مليار شخص بيستعمل يوتيوب كل شهر، و عشان كده ممكن ينافس تيك توك.

في إبريل ٢٠١٩، جرنال التلجراف قال إن المعلنين كانوا بيدفعوا للناس ٦٠٠-١٠٠٠ دولار في البوست الواحد لو كان عندهم من مليون لاتنين مليون متابع على تيك توك. تمن المنشور اللي زي ده على إنستاجرام ما بين ١٠,٠٠٠ و ١٢,٠٠٠ دولار.

'Shorts' Feature on YouTube to Compete With TikTok

Key Words

الكلمات

Study the key words and their definitions.

Translations	Definitions	Key Words
____________	بيِشْتغل دِلْوَقْتي	شغّال
____________	حاجة مُميّزة في حاجة	خاصّية
____________	عاز يبْقى أحْسن مِن حدّ تاني	نافِس (يِنافِس)
____________	شخْص أوْ شِرْكة بيِدْفع فلوس عشان النّاس يِعْرفوه	مُعْلِن / مُعْلِنة
____________	منْشور	پوسْت
____________	حدّ بيِشوف حدّ على السوْشال ميدِيا	مُتابِع / مُتابْعة
____________	سِعْر	تمن (أتْمان)

Now match these translations to the key words above. Check your answers in the answer key.

feature • follower • post • price; value • sponsor; advertiser • to compete • working

The Article

المقالة

1 خاصّيةْ **شورْتْس** على يوتْيوب هتْنافِس **تيك توْك**

2 فيه أخْبار إنّ **يوتْيوب** دِلْوَقْتي شغّال على خاصّية جِديدة إسْمها **شورْتْش** عشان يِنافِس بيها **تيك توْك**.

3 النّاس مُمْكِن يِعْمِلوا على **تيك توْك** ڤيدْيوهات خمسْتاشر ثانْيَة.

4 تمانين في المية مِن اللي بِيِسْتعمِلوا **تيك توْك** في الوِلايات المتّحِدة أعْمارْهُم مِن سِتّاشر لِأرْبعة و تلاتين سنة.

5 **تيك توْك** بدأ في الصّين في ألْفيْن و سِتّاشر، و أكْتر مِن مِلْيار شخْص بِيِسْتعمِلوه كُلّ شهْر.

6 بسّ فيه اِتْنيْن مِلْيار شخْص بِيِسْتعْمِل **يوتْيوب** كُلّ شهْر، و عشان كِده مُمْكِن يِنافِس **تيك توْك**.

7 في إبْريل ألْفيْن و تِسعْتاشر، جُرْنال **التِّلِجْراف** قال إنّ المُعْلِنين كانوا بِيِدْفعوا لِلنّاس مِن سُتّمية لِألْف دولار في البوسْت الواحِد لَوْ كان عنْدُهُم مِن مِلْيوْن لِاتْنيْن مِلْيوْن مُتابِع على **تيك توْك**.

8 تمن المنْشور اللي زيّ ده على **إنْسْتاجْرام** ما بيْن عشرْتلاف و اِتْناشر ألْف دولار.

أسئلة الفهم Comprehension Questions

١. فيه كام شخْص بيِسْتعْمِل **تيك توْك** كُلّ شهْر؟

٢. مُعْظم اللي بيِسْتعْمِلوا **تيك توْك** شباب؟

٣. ليْه **يوتْيوب** عايِز يِعْمِل خاصّية **شورْتْس**؟

أسئلة المناقشة Discussion Questions

٤. أيْه رأْيَك في خاصّيةْ **شورْتْس**؟

٥. عنْدك **تيك توْك**؟ أيْه رأْيَك فيه؟

٦. بِتْحِبّ تِتْفرّج على أيْه على الإنْترْنِت؟

٧. تِحِبّ تِبْقى مشْهور؟ ليْه؟

٨. هل إنْتَ شخْص بيْحِبّ المُنافْسة؟

Expressions and Structures تعبيرات و تراكيب

Try to remember the Arabic expressions and structures from the article. Each English translation is followed by four choices, only one of which is correct. Refer back to the article to check your answers.

1. **a feature called "Shorts"**

خاصّية بِالإسْم شورْتْش	خاصّية اللي إسْمها شورْتْش
خاصّية إسْمها شورْتْش	خاصّية مِسمّية شورْتْش

2. **more than a billion people**

أكْتر مِن مِلْيار أشْخاص	أكْتر مِلْيار شخْص
شخْسينْ أكْتر مِن مِلْيار	أكْتر مِن مِلْيار شخْص

3. **every month**

كُلّ الشُّهور	كُلّ شهْر
كُلُّه شهْر	كُلّ الشّهْر

4. **on TikTok**

على تيك توْك	فوْق تيك توْك
عن تيك توْك	بِتيك توْك

Answer Key and Translations

الإجابات و الترجمات

Key Word Answers

working شغّال • feature خاصّية • to compete نافِس • sponsor; advertiser مُعْلِن • post پوسْت • follower مُتابِع • price; value تمن

Translation of the Article

1. **'Shorts' Feature on YouTube to Compete With Tiktok**
2. {There is news that} YouTube is now working on a new feature called 'Shorts' to compete with TikTok.
3. People can make 15-second videos on TikTok.
4. Eighty percent of those who use TikTok in the US {their ages} are between 16 and 34 years old.
5. TikTok started in China in 2016, and more than a billion people {person} use it every month.
6. But there are two billion people {person} who use YouTube every month, and that's why it can compete with TikTok.
7. In April 2019, {the newspaper of} The Telegraph said that advertisers were paying people $600-$1000 per post if they had between one and two million followers on Tiktok.
8. The price of such a post on Instagram is between $10,000 and $12,000.

Phonemic Transcription of the Article

1. *xaṣṣíyyit [Shorts] 3ála [YouTube] hatnāfis tīk tōk*
2. *fī ʔaxbār ʔinnə [YouTube] dilwáʔti šaɣɣāl 3ála xaṣṣíyya g(i)dīda ʔismáha [Shorts] 3ašān yināfis bīha [TikTok].*
3. *innās múmkin yi3mílu 3ála [TikTok] vidyuhāt xamastāšar sánya.*
4. *tamanīn fi -lmíyya min ílli byista3ímalu [TikTok] fi -lwilayāt ilmuttáɦida ʔa3márhum min sittāšar li-ʔarbá3a w talatīn sána.*
5. *[TikTok] bádaʔ fi -ṣṣīn fi ʔalafēn wi sittāšar, wi ʔáktar min milyār šaxṣ(ə) b(i)yista3imalū kullə šahr.*
6. *bassə fī ʔitnēn milyār šaxṣ(ə) b(i)yistá3mil [YouTube] kullə šahr, wi 3ašān kída múmkin yināfis [TikTok].*
7. *fi ʔibrīl ʔalfēn wi tis3tāšar, gurnāl it[Telegraph] ʔāl ʔinn ilmu3linīn kānu b(i)yidfá3u li-nnās min suttumīt li-ʔalfə dulār fi -l[post] ilwāɦid law kān 3andúhum min milyōn li-tnēn milyōn mutābi3 3ála tīk tōk.*

8. *táman ilmanšūr ílli zayyə da 3ála [Instagram] ma bēn 3ašartalāf w itnāšar ʔalf(ə) dulār.*

Translation of the Questions

1. How many monthly users does TikTok have? 2. Are the majority of those who use TikTok young people? 3. Why does YouTube want to make a "Shorts" feature? 4. What is your opinion of the "Shorts" feature? 5. Do you have TikTok? What is your opinion of it? 6. What do you like to watch on the internet? 7. Would you like to be famous? Why (not)? 8. Are you a competitive person?

Answers to Expressions and Structures

1. a feature called "Shorts" خاصّية إسْمها شورْتْش
2. more than a billion people أكْتر مِن مِلْيار شخْص
3. every month كُلّ شهْر
4. on TikTok على تيك توْك

Notes

چي كي رولينج نشرت كتاب جديد مجاني أونلاين

چي كي رولينج نشرت حدوتة جديدة إسمها ذي إيكابوج و اللي هتكون مجانية أونلاين عشان تسلي الأطفال و العائلات اللي قاعدين في البيت.

كاتبة هاري پوتر قالت إنها كتبت الحدوتة دي من ١٠ سنين عشان تبقى حدوتة قبل النوم لأطفالها. الحدوتة بتدور أحداثها في أرض خيالية. الحدوتة معمولة عشان الأطفال اللي أعمارهم من ٧ لـ٩ سنين.

رولينج كتبت على موقعها الإلكتروني: "الحدوتة دي مش هاري پوتر و مفيهاش سحر... دي قصة مختلفة خالص."

رولينج طلبت برضه من الأطفال إنهم يبعتوا رسوماتهم ، و فيه فرصة إن رسوماتهم تظهر على النسخة المطبوعة من الكتاب.

الكتاب هيتنشر في نوڤمبر. رولينج قالت إنها هتتبرع بكل الفلوس اللي هتيجي من المبيعات عشان تساعد الناس اللي اتضروا بوباء كورونا.

J.K. Rowling Releases Free New Book Online

Key Words | الكلمات

Study the key words and their definitions.

Translations	Definitions	Key Words
________	خلّى النّاس يِقْدروا يشوفوا كِتاب أَوْ أيّ منْشور	نشر (يِنْشُر)
________	قِصّة	حدّوتة (حَواديت)
________	بِبلاش؛ مِن غيرْ فِلوس	مجّاني
________	ساعِد شخْص إنُّه مَيْكونْش زهْقان	سلّى (يِسلّي)
________	مِش حقيقي	خَيالي
________	قُوّة غريبة مُمْكِن تِغيرّ الحاجات	سِحْر
________	صورة معْمولة بِالإيد	رسْمة (رُسومات)
________	بان	ظهر (يِظْهر)
________	المبْني لِلمجْهول مِن "نشر"	اِتْنشر (يِتْنِشِر)
________	إدّى حاجة مِن غيرْ مُقابِل مادّي	اِتْبرّع (يِتْبرّع)

Now match these translations to the key words above. Check your answers in the answer key.

drawing; painting • fictional • free (of cost) • imaginative story; children's story, fairy tale • magic • to appear • to be published • to donate • to entertain • to publish

The Article المقالة

1 **چيْ كيْ روْلينْج** نشرِت كِتاب جِديد مجّاني أونْلايْن

2 **چيْ كيْ روْلينْج** نشرِت حدّوتة جِديدة إسْمها **ذي إيكابوْج** و اللي هتْكون مجّانية أونْلايْن عشان تِسلّي الأطْفال و العائِلات اللي قاعْدين في البيْت.

3 كاتِبةْ **هاري پوْتر** قالِت إنّها كتبِت الحدّوتة دي مِن عشر سِنين عشان تِبْقى حدّوتِةْ قبْل النّوْم لِأطْفالْها.

4 الحدّوتة بِتْدور أحْداثْها في أرْض خَيالية.

5 الحدّوتة معْمولة عشان الأطْفال اللي أعْمارْهُم مِن سبع لِتِسع سِنين.

6 **روْلينْج** كتبِت على مَوْقِعْها الإلِكْتروْني: "الحدّوتة دي مِش **هاري پوْتر** و مفيهاش سِحْر... دي قِصّة مُخْتلِفة خالِص."

7 **روْلينْج** طلبِت برْضُه مِن الأطْفال إنّهُم يِبْعتوا رُسوماتْهُم، و فيه فُرْصة إنّ رُسوماتْهُم تِظْهر على النُّسْخة المطْبوعة مِن الكِتاب.

8 الكِتاب هَيِتْنِشِر في نوڤمْبِر.

9 **روْلينْج** قالِت إنّها هتِتْبرّع بِكُلّ الفِلوس اللي هتيجي مِن المبيعات عشان تِساعِد النّاس اللي اِتْضرّوا بِوَباء كوروْنا.

Comprehension Questions أسئلة الفهم

١. الحّدوتة الجِديدة اِتْنشرِت أونْلايْن بِكام؟

٢. أيْه علاقِةْ **ذي إيكابوْج بِهاري پوْتر؟**

٣. **روْلينْج** كتبِت الحدّوتة دي ليْه؟

Discussion Questions أسئلة المناقشة

٤. أيْه رأْيَك في الحدّوتة الجِديدة؟

٥. بِتْحِبّ **هاري پوْتر؟** لَوْ آه، بِتْحِبّ الكُتُب أكْتر وَلّا الأفْلام؟ لَوْ لأ، ليْه؟

٦. بِتْحِبّ القِرايَة؟ ليْه؟

٧. أيْه أكْتر حاجة كُنْت بِتْحِبّ تِعْمِلْها لمّا كُنْت طِفْل؟

٨. لَوْ هتِكْتِب كِتاب لِلأطْفال، هتِكْتِبُه عن أيْه؟

Expressions and Structures تعبيرات و تراكيب

Try to remember the Arabic expressions and structures from the article. Each English translation is followed by four choices, only one of which is correct. Refer back to the article to check your answers.

1. **the story is made for kids**

   الحدّوتة معْمولة عشان الأطْفال

   الحدّوتة المعْمولة لِأطْفال

   الحدّوتة عِبارة عن الأطْفال

   الحدّوتة بِتْكون معْمولة مِن الأطْفال

2. **an entirely different story**

   قِصّة مُخْتلِفة خالْصة

   قِصّة مُخْتلِفة خلاص

   قِصّة مُخْتلِفة خالِص

   قِصّة مُخْتلِفة خاصّةً

3. **she asked children to...**

   طلبِت مِن الأطْفال إنُّهْم

   سألِت الأطْفال لِـ

   طلبِت الأطْفال عشان

   سألِت بِالأطْفال إنُّهْم

4. **she will donate all of the money**

   هتِتْبرّع كُلّ الفِلوس

   هتْبرّع بِكُلّ الفِلوس

   هتِتْبرّع بِكُلّ الفِلوس

   هتْبرّع كُلّ الفِلوس

Answer Key and Translations

الإجابات و الترجمات

Key Word Answers

to publish نشر • imaginative story; children's story, fairy tale حدّوتة • free (of cost) مجّاني • to entertain سلّى • fictional خَيالي • magic سِحْر • drawing; painting رسْمة • to appear ظهر • to be published اِتْنشر • to donate اِتْبرّع

Translation of the Article

1. **J.K. Rowling Releases Free New Book Online**
2. J.K. Rowling has published a new story called The Ickabog, which will be free online to entertain kids and families who are staying home [during the pandemic].
3. The writer of Harry Potter said that she wrote this story ten years ago to be a bedtime story for her kids.
4. The story takes place in an imaginary land.
5. The story is made for kids who {whose ages} are from seven to nine years old.
6. Rowling wrote on her website, "It {this} (the story) is not Harry Potter, and it does not include magic... This is an entirely different story."
7. Rowling also asked {from the} kids to send their drawings, and there is a chance that their drawings appear on the paperback version of the book.
8. The books will be published in November.
9. Rowling said she would donate all the money that will come from the sales to help those who have been affected {harmed} by the coronavirus pandemic.

Phonemic Transcription of the Article

1. *[J.K. Rowling] nášarit kitāb gidīd maggāni [online]*
2. *[J.K. Rowling] nášarit ḫaddūta gdīda ʔismáha [The Ickabog] w ílli hatkūn magganíyya [online] 3ašān tisálli -lʔaṭfāl w il3aʔilāt ílli ʔa3dīn fi -lbēt.*
3. *kātíbit [Harry Potter] ʔālit ʔinnáha kátabit ilḫaddūta di min 3ášar sinīn 3ašān tíbʔa ḫaddūtit ʔabl innōm li-ʔaṭfálha.*

4. *ilḫaddūta bitdūr ʔaḫdásha f(i) ʔarḍ(ə) xayalíyya.*
5. *ilḫaddūta ma3mūla 3ašān ilʔaṭfāl ílli ʔa3márhum min sába3 li-tísa3 sinīn.*
6. *[Rowling] kátabit 3ála mawqí3ha (i)lʔiliktrōni: "ilḫaddūta di miš [Harry Potter] wi ma-fihāš siḫr... di qíṣṣa muxtálifa xāliṣ."*
7. *[Rowling] ṭálabit bárḍu min ilʔaṭfāl ʔinnúhum yib3átu rusumáthum, wi fī fúrṣa ʔinnə rusumáthum tíẓhar 3ála (i)nnúsxa (i)lmaṭbū3a min ilkitāb.*
8. *ilkitāb hayitníšir fi nuvámbir.*
9. *[Rowling] ʔālit ʔinnáha hatitbárra3 bi-kúll ilfilūs ílli hatīgi min ilmabi3āt 3ašān tisā3id innās ílli -tḍḍáru b(i)-wabāʔ kurōna.*

Translation of the Questions

1. How much [at what price] will the story be published online for? 2. What is the relationship/connection between The Ickabog and Harry Potter [stories]? 3. Why did Rowling write this story? 4. What do you think about the new story? 5. Do you like Harry Potter? If so, do you like the books better or the movies? If not, why [not]? 6. Do you like reading? Why (not)? 7. What was your favorite thing to do when you were a kid? 8. If you were going to write a book for children, what would you write about?

Answers to Expressions and Structures

1. the story is made for kids الحدّوتة معْمولة عشان الأطْفال
2. an entirely different story قِصّة مُخْتلِفة خالِص
3. she asked children to... طلبِت مِن الأطْفال إنُّهْم
4. she will donate all of the money هتِتْبرّع بِكُلّ الفلوس

Notes

مركب و عجلة و بيت في نفس الوقت

شركة زلتيني عملت وسيلة مواصلات بتمشي على الأرض و الماية و فيها مكان للنوم.

الزي تريتون عبارة عن مركب و عجلة و بيت صغير أوي في نفس الوقت. الشركة بتقول إنها ممكن تستعمل في الرحلات الطويلة و القصيرة، و فيها مكان لشخصين.

الزي تريتون طولها ٣.٦ من عشرة متر و عرضها ١.٢ من عشرة متر. تمنها هيكون من ٨٠٠٠ لـ١٠,٠٠٠ دولار. الناس ممكن يشتروا واحدة جاهزة أو يعملوا واحدة بنفسهم.

صاحب شركة زلتيني مشي بعجلته ٣٠ ألف كيلو من لندن لطوكيو في أكتر من ٤ سنين، بس محبش ينام في خيمة و مقدرش يعدي الماية بالعجلة بس. عشان كده، قرر يعمل الزي تريتون اللي كمان بتستعمل طاقة شمسية عشان تكون كويسة للبيئة.

١٤ Boat, Bike and House at the Same Time

Key Words الكلمات

Study the key words and their definitions.

Translations	Definitions	Key Words
______	أيّ حاجة مُمْكِن الإنْسان يروح بيها مِن مكان لِمكان	وَسيلةْ مُواصْلات (وَسايِل مُواصْلات)
______	المبْني لِلمجْهول مِن "اِسْتَعمِل"	اِستُعْمِل (يُستعْمل)
______	الضِّلْع الأطْوَل مِن ضِلْعيْن أوْ تلاتة مِن شكْل هندسي	طول
______	الضِّلْع الأقْصر مِن ضِلْعيْن أوْ تلاتة مِن شكْل هندسي	عرْض
______	مُمْكِن يُسْتعْمل على طول	جاهِز
______	عِرِف يعْمِل حاجة	قِدِر (يِقْدر)
______	مِشي مِن ناحْيَة لِلتّانْيَة	عدّى (يِعَدّي)
______	الطّبيعة	البيئة

Now match these translations to the key words above. Check your answers in the answer key.

length • means of transport • ready • the environment • to be able to • to be used • to cross • width

The Article المقالة

1 مركِب و عجلة و بيْت في نفْس الوَقْت

2 شرِكِةْ **زِلْتيني** عملِت وَسيلِةْ مُواصْلات بتِمْشي على الأرْض و المايّة و فيها مكان لِلنّوْم.

3 **الزّي تْرَيْتوْن** عِبارة عن مركِب و عجلة و بيْت صُغيرّ أوي في نفْس الوَقْت.

4 الشِّرْكة بِتْقول إنّها مُمْكِن تُسْتعْمل في الرّحلات الطَّويلة و القُصيرّة، و فيها مكان لِشخْصينْ.

5 **الزّي تْرَيْتوْن** طولْها تلاتة و ستّة مِن عشرة مِتْر و عرْضها واحِد و اِتْنيْن مِن عشرة مِتْر.

6 تمنْها هَيْكون مِن تمانْتلاف لِعشرْتلاف دولار.

7 النّاس مُمْكِن يِشْتروا واحْدة جاهْزة أَوْ يِعْملوا واحْدة بِنفْسُهم.

8 صاحِب شرِكِةْ **زِلْتيني** مِشي بِعجلْتُه تلاتين ألْف كيلو مِن **لنْدن لِطوكْيو** في أكْتر مِن أرْبع سِنين،

9 بسّ محبِّش يِنام في خيْمة و مقْدرْش يِعدّي المايّة بِالعجلة بسّ.

10 عشان كِده، قرّر يِعْمِل **الزّي تْرَيْتوْن** اللي كمان بِتِسْتعْمِل طاقة شمْسية عشان تِكون كُوَيِّسة لِلبيئة.

أسئلة الفهم Comprehension Questions

١. **الزّي تْرَيْتوْن** بِكام؟
٢. مُمْكِن حدّ يِنام في **الزّي تْرَيْتوْن**؟
٣. ليْه صاحِب زِلْتيني قرّر يِعْمِل **الزّي تْرَيْتوْن**؟

أسئلة المناقشة Discussion Questions

٤. أيْه رأْيَك في **الزّي تْرَيْتوْن**؟
٥. مُمْكِن تِفكّر تِشْتِري **الزّي تْرَيْتوْن**؟ ليْه؟
٦. هل إنْتَ شخْص بِتْحِبّ المُغامْرة؟
٧. أيْه أكْتر وَسيلِةْ مُواصْلات بِتْحِبّها؟
٨. تِفْتِكِر كُلّ حاجة في المُسْتقْبل هتِسْتعْمِل طاقة شمْسية؟ ليْه شايِف كِده؟

Expressions and Structures تعبيرات و تراكيب

Try to remember the Arabic expressions and structures from the article. Each English translation is followed by four choices, only one of which is correct. Refer back to the article to check your answers.

1. **The Zeltini company**

الزِلْتيني شرِكة

الشِّرْكة مِن **زِلْتيني**

الشِّرْكة **لِزِلْتيني**

شِرْكِةْ **زِلْتيني**

2. **it can accommodate two people**

مكانُه عِبارة عن شخْصينْ

فيها مكان لِشخْصينْ

في مكانُه عشان شخْصينْ

مكانُه لِشخْصينْ

3. **3.6 (three point six)**

تلاتة نُقْطة ستّة

تلاتة و سِتّة مِن عشرة

تلاتة على سِتّة

تلاتة و سِتّة في عشرة

4. **he decided to make**

قرّر عشان يِعْمِل

قرّر إنُّه عمل

قرّر يِعْمِل

قرّر بيِعْمِل

Answer Key and Translations الإجابات و الترجمات

Key Word Answers

means of transport وَسيلةْ مُواصْلات • to be used اِستُعْمِل • length طول • width عرْض • ready جاهِز • to be able to قِدِر • to cross عدّى • the environment البيئة

Translation of the Article

1. **Boat, Bike and House at the Same Time**
2. The company Zeltini has made a vehicle that travels {moves} on land and water and has a place to sleep in it.
3. The Z-Triton is a boat, bicycle, and a very small house at the same time.
4. The company says it can be used on long and short trips, and it can accommodate {has in it} room for two people.
5. The Z-Triton {its length} is 3.6 meters long and {its width} is 1.2 meters wide.
6. It will cost {its cost will be} $8,000-$10,000.
7. People can buy one ready or assemble {make} one by themselves.
8. The owner of Zeltini traveled by {his} bicycle 30,000 km from London to Tokyo in over four years,
9. but he did not like to sleep in a tent and could not cross water just by bicycle.
10. Because of that, he decided to make the Z-Triton, which also uses solar power to be good for the environment.

Phonemic Transcription of the Article

1. *márkib wi 3ágala wi bēt fi nafs ilwáʔt*
2. *šírkit [Zeltini] 3ámalit wasīlit muwaşlāt bitímši 3ála -lʔarɖ(ə) w ilmáyya wi fīha makān li-nnōm.*
3. *íz-[Z-Triton] 3ibāra 3an márkib wi 3ágala w(i) bēt şuɣáyyar ʔáwi f(i) nafs ilwáʔt.*
4. *iššírka bitʔūl ʔinnáha múmkin tustá3mal fi -rraɦalāt iţţawīla w ilʔuşayyára, wi fīha makān li-šaxşēn.*
5. *íz-[Z-Triton] ţúlha talāta w(i) sítta min 3ášara mitr(ə) w(i) 3arɖáha wāɦid w itnēn min 3ášara mitr.*

6. *tamánha haykūn min tamantalāf li-3ašartalāf dulār.*
7. *innās múmkin yištíru wáɦda gáhza ʔaw yi3mílu wáɦda b(i)-nafsúhum.*
8. *ṣāɦib šírkit [Zeltini] míši bi-3agáltu talatīn ʔalfə kīlu min lándan li-ṭúkyu f(i) ʔáktar min ʔárba3 sinīn,*
9. *bassə ma-ɦábbiš yinām fi xēma wi ma-ʔdíršə y(i)3áddi -lmáyya bi-l3ágala bass.*
10. *3ašān kída, qárrar yí3mil íz-[Z-Triton] ílli kamān bitistá3mil ṭāqa šamsíyya 3ašān tikūn kuwayyísa li-lbīʔa.*

Translation of the Questions

1. How much does the Z-Triton cost? 2. Can someone sleep in the Z-Triton? 3. Why did the owner of Ziltini decide to make the Z-Triton? 4. What is your opinion of the Z-Triton? 5. Would you ever consider buying a Z-Triton? Why (not)? 6. Are you an adventurous person? 7. What is your favorite mode of transport? 8. Do you think everything in the future will use solar power? Why do you think so?

Answers to Expressions and Structures

1. The Zeltini company شِرْكِةْ زِلْتيني
2. it can accommodate two people فيها مكان لِشخْصين
3. 3.6 (three point six) تلاتة و سِتّة مِن عشرة
4. he decided to make قِرّر يِعْمِل

Notes

دراسة: بدأ اليوم الدراسي متأخر أحسن

فيه دراسة في ٢٠١٧ اتعملت على مدرسة ثانوية في إنجلترا لقت إن الطلاب اللي بدأوا اليوم الدراسي الساعة ١٠:٠٠ الصبح بدل ٨:٥٠ كانت صحتهم و درجاتهم أحسن.

في السنة الأولى، الطلاب بدأوا اليوم الدراسي الساعة ٨:٥٠ الصبح. في السنة التانية و التالتة، الوقت اتغير لـ١٠:٠٠ الصبح. بعد كده في السنة الرابعة، الطلاب رجعوا تاني يبدأوا الساعة ٨:٥٠ الصبح.

الباحثين بصوا على نسبة الغياب لأسباب صحية، و على درجات الطلاب في المدرسة. في السنتين اللي الطلاب راحوا المدرسة فيهم متأخر، نسبة الغياب قلت و الدرجات زادت.

الأستاذ الجامعي راسل فوستر من جامعة أوكسفورد بيقول إن المراهقين محتاجين ٩ ساعات نوم، بس كتير منهم بيناموا ٥ ساعات بس في أيام الدراسة.

١٥ Study: Starting School Day Late Is Better

Key Words — الكلمات

Study the key words and their definitions.

Translations	Definitions	Key Words
____________	كبديل عن	بدل
____________	حالةْ الجِسْم	صِحّة
____________	أداء الطّالِب الدِّراسي	درجة
____________	عمل حاجة لِأوِّل مرّة	بدأ (يِبْدأ)
____________	يوْم في المدْرسة	يوْم دِراسي (أيّام دِراسية)
____________	بدأ يِعْمِل حاجة تاني	رِجِع (يِرْجع)
____________	عكْس حُضور	غِياب
____________	عكْس بدْري	مِتْأخّر
____________	بقى أكْتر	زاد (يِزيد)
____________	بقى أقلّ	قلّ (يِقِلّ)

Now match these translations to the key words above. Check your answers in the answer key.

absence • grade • health • instead of • late • school day • to decrease, go down • to increase, go up • to return, go back • to start

The Article المقالة

1 دِراسة: بدْأ اليوْم الدِّراسي متْأخّر أحْسن

2 فيه دِراسة في ألْفين و سبعْتاشر اِتْعملِت على مدْرسة ثانَوية في إنْجِلْترا لقِت إنّ الطُّلّاب اللي بدأوا اليوْم الدِّراسي السّاعة عشرة الصُّبْح بدل تِسْعة إلّا عشرة كانِت صِحِّتْهُم و درجاتْهُم أحْسن.

3 في السّنة الأولى، الطُّلّاب بدأوا اليوْم الدِّراسي السّاعة تِسْعة إلّا عشرة الصُّبْح.

4 في السّنة التّانْيَة و التّالْتة، الوَقْت اِتْغيرّ لِعشرة الصُّبْح.

5 بعْد كِده في السّنة الرّابْعة، الطُّلّاب رِجْعوا تاني يِبْدأوا السّاعة تِسْعة إلّا عشرة الصُّبْح.

6 الباحِثين بصّوا على نِسْبِةْ الغِياب لِأسْباب صِحّية، و على درجات الطُّلّاب في المدْرسة.

7 في السّنتينْ اللي الطُّلّاب راحوا المدْرسة فيهُم مِتْأخّر، نِسْبِةْ الغِياب قلِّت و الدّرجات زادِت.

8 الأُسْتاذ الجامِعي **راسل فوسْتر** مِن جامْعِةْ **أوكْسْفورْد** بِيْقول إنّ المُراهْقين محْتاجين تِسع ساعات نوْم، بسّ كِتير مِنْهُم بِيْناموا خمس ساعات بسّ في أيّام الدِّراسة.

Comprehension Questions أسئلة الفهم

١. الدُّكْتور **راسل فوسْتر** بِيْقول إنّ المُراهْقين المفْروض يِناموا كام ساعة في اليوْم؟

٢. الدِّراسة دي اِتْعملِت فيْن؟

٣. لمّا الطُّلّاب بدأوا متْأخّر، الغِياب لِأسْباب صِحّية قلّ وَلّا زاد؟

Discussion Questions أسئلة المناقشة

٤. أيْه رأْيَك في نتايِج الدِّراسة دي؟

٥. بِتْنام كام ساعة في اليوْم؟ إنْتَ شايِف إنّ ده كِفايَة وَلّا لأ؟

٦. لمّا كُنْت في المدْرسة، كان اليوْم الدِّراسي بِيِبْدأ إمْتى؟

٧. كُنْت بِتْغيب كِتير مِن المدْرسة؟

٨. لمّا بِتِصْحى، بِتِفْتِكِر الأحْلام اللي شُفْتها لمّا كُنْت نايِم؟

Expressions and Structures تعبيرات و تراكيب

Try to remember the Arabic expressions and structures from the article. Each English translation is followed by four choices, only one of which is correct. Refer back to the article to check your answers.

1. **the school day**

الأيّام الدِّراسي

يوْم المدْرسي

يوْم المدْراسة

اليوْم الدِّراسي

2. **8:50 (ten to nine)**

عشرة لِساعةْ تِسْعة

تِسع ساعة و عشرة

عشرة إلّا السّاعة تِسْعة

السّاعة تِسْعة إلّا عشرة

3. **they looked at the absence rate**

دوّروا على نِسْبِةْ الغِياب

بصّوا نِسْبِةْ الغِياب

شافوا في نِسْبِةْ الغِياب

بصّوا على نِسْبِةْ الغِياب

4. **nine hours of sleep**

تِسع ساعات نوْم

تِسْعة ساعات النّوْم

تِسع ساعة مِنْ النّوْم

السّاعة تِسْعة نوْم

Answer Key and Translations

الإجابات و الترجمات

Key Word Answers

instead of بدل • health صحّة • grade درجة • to start بدأ • school day يوْم دِراسي • to return, go back رِجِع • absence غِياب • late مِتْأخّر • to increase, go up زاد • to decrease, go down قلّ

Translation of the Article

1. **Study: Starting School Day Late Is Better**
2. A study from 2017 that was done on a high school in England found that students who started the school day at 10:00 a.m. {in the morning} instead of 8:50 {nine except/minus ten [minutes]} had better health and their grades were better.
3. In first grade {year}, the students started the school day at 8:50 a.m.
4. In second and third grade, the time changed to 10 a.m.
5. After that, in fourth grade, the students went back again to starting at 8:50 a.m.
6. The researchers looked at the absence rate for health reasons and at the grades of students at school.
7. In the two years in which the students went to school late, the absence rate decreased, and [their] grades went up.
8. Professor Russell Foster from Oxford University says that teenagers need nine hours of sleep, but many of them only sleep five hours on school days.

Phonemic Transcription of the Article

1. *dirāsa: badʔ ilyōm iddirāsi mitʔáxxar ʔáḫsan*
2. *fī dirāsa f(i) ʔalfēn wi saba3tāšar it3ámalit 3ála madrása sanawíyya f(i) ʔingiltára láʔit ʔinn iṭṭullāb ílli bádaʔu -lyōm iddirāsi (i)ssā3a 3ášara iṣṣúbḫ, bádal tís3a ílla 3ášara, kānit ṣiḫḫíthum wi daragáthum ʔáḫsan.*
3. *fi -ssána -lʔūla, iṭṭullāb bádaʔu -lyōm iddirāsi (i)ssā3a tís3a ílla 3ášara -ṣṣúbḫ.*
4. *fi -ssána ittánya w ittálta, ilwáʔt itɣáyyar li-3ášara -ṣṣúbḫ.*
5. *ba3də kída fi -ssána irráb3a, iṭṭullāb ríg3u tāni yibdáʔu (i)ssā3a tís3a ílla 3ášara (i)ṣṣúbḫ.*

6. *ilbaɦisīn báṣṣu 3ála nísbit ilɣiyāb li-ʔasbāb ṣiɦɦíyya, wi 3ála daragāt iṭṭullāb fi -lmadrása.*
7. *fi -ssanatēn ílli -ṭṭullāb rāɦu -lmadrása fīhum mitʔáxxar, nísbit ilɣiyāb ʔállit w iddaragāt zādit.*
8. *ilʔustāz ilgāmí3i [Russell Foster] min gám3it [Oxford] biyʔūl ʔinn ilmurahqīn miɦtagīn tísa3 sa3āt nōm, bassə ktīr mínhum biynāmu xámas sa3āt bass(ə) f(i) ʔayyām iddirāsa.*

Translation of the Questions

1. How many hours a night {day} does Professor Russell Foster say teenagers should sleep? 2. When was this study done? 3. When students started later, did the absence rate for health reasons go down or up? 4. What is your opinion of this study's results? 5. How many hours a night do you sleep? Do you think that this is enough? 6. When you were in school, when did the school day start? 7. Where you absent from school a lot? 8. When you wake up, do you remember the dreams you had while sleeping?

Answers to Expressions and Structures

1. the school day اليوْم الدِّراسي
2. 8:50 (ten to nine) السّاعة تِسْعة إلّا عشرة
3. they looked at the absence rate بصّوا على نِسْبِةْ الغِياب
4. nine hours of sleep تِسع ساعات نوْم

Notes

اكتشاف: بكتيريا جديدة بتاكل البلاستك

فيه باحثين اكتشفوا بكتيريا جديدة بتاكل نوع من البلاستك إسمه "پوليوريثين". النوع ده صعب يتعاد تدويره.

فيه علما بيقولوا إن الاكتشاف ده ممكن يقلل كمية البلاستك اللي بتترمي في مقالب الزبالة و المحيطات.

فريق من مركز أبحاث في ألمانيا، لقى نوع البكتيريا ده في منطقة كان فيها كميات ضخمة من البلاستك. الفريق لقى إن البكتيريا بتنتج إنزيمات بتكسر البوليوريثين.

البحث الألماني بيقول إن العلما ممكن يتحكموا في البكتيريا دي بسهولة و ينتجوها للاستخدامات الصناعية. بس بعض الباحثين بيقولوا إننا محتاجين أبحاث أكتر قبل ما نحط البكتيريا دي في بيئات طبيعية.

الإنسان بينتج حوالي ٣٠٠ مليون طن بلاستك كل سنة. حوالي نص الكمية دي بتستعمل مرة واحدة بس، و حوالي ٨ مليون طن بلاستك بيترموا في المحيطات.

١٦ Discovery: New Bacteria Eats Plastic

Key Words — الكلمات

Study the key words and their definitions.

Translations	Definitions	Key Words
____________	عِرِف حاجة جِديدة	اِكْتَشَف (يِكْتِشِف)
____________	حاجة اِكْتُشِفت؛ حاجة اِتْعرفِت لأوِّل مرّة	اِكْتِشاف
____________	مكان كِبير بِتِترِمي فيه زِبالة	مقْلب زِبالة (مقالِب زِبالة)
____________	سطْح كِبير أوي مِن المايّة، أكْبر مِن البحْر	مُحيط
____________	المبْنى لِلمجْهول مِن "رمى"	اِتْرمى (يِترِمي)
____________	مجْموعة بِتِعْمِل حاجة واحْدة مع بعْض	فريق (فِرق)
____________	عمل حاجة	أنْتج (يِنْتِج)
____________	دِراسة؛ أُسْلوب مُنظّم في جمْع المعْلومات	بَحْث (أَبْحاث)
____________	خلّى حدّ أَوْ حاجة تِعْمِل اللي هُوَّ عايْزه	اِتْحكِّم (يِتْحكِّم)
____________	مِقْدار	كِمّية

Now match these translations to the key words above. Check your answers in the answer key.

amount • discovery • landfill • ocean • research, study • team • to be thrown; be dumped • to control • to discover • to produce

The Article المقالة

1 اكْتِشاف: بكْتيرِيا جِديدة بِتاكُل البلاسْتِك

2 فيه باحِثين اكْتشفوا بكْتيرِيا جِديدة بِتاكُل نوْع مِن البلاسْتِك إسْمُه "پولِيوريثيْن."

3 النّوْع ده صعْب يِتْعاد تدْويرُه.

4 فيه عُلما بِيْقولوا إنّ الاكْتِشاف ده مُمْكِن يِقلِّل كمِّيّة البلاسْتِك اللي بِتِترِمي في مقالِب الزِّبالة و المُحيطات.

5 فريق مِن مرْكز أبْحاث في ألْمانْيا، لقى نوْع البكْتيرِيا ده في منْطِقة كان فيها كمِّيات ضخْمة مِن البلاسْتِك.

6 الفريق لقى إنّ البكْتيرِيا بِتِنْتِج إنْزيمْات بِتْكسّر البولِيوريثيْن.

7 البحْث الألْماني بِيْقول إنّ العُلما مُمْكِن يِتْحكِّموا في البكْتيرِيا دي بِسْهولة و يِنْتِجوها لِلاِسْتِخْدامات الصِّناعية.

8 بسّ بعْض الباحِثين بِيْقولوا إنِّنا محْتاجين أبْحاث أكْتر قبْل ما نحُطّ البكْتيرِيا دي في بيئات طبيعية.

9 الإنْسان بِيِنْتِج حَوالي تُلْتُمية مِلْيوْن طِنّ بلاسْتِك كُلّ سنة.

10 حَوالي نُصّ الكمِّية دي بِتُسْتعْمل مرّة واحْدة بسّ، و حَوالي تمانْيَة مِلْيوْن طِنّ بِلاسْتِك بِيِترِموا في المُحيطات.

أسئلة الفهم Comprehension Questions

١. مين اِكْتشف الاكْتِشاف ده؟

٢. الإنْسان بيِنْتِج بلاسْتِك قدّ أيْه كُلّ سنة؟

٣. الإنْسان مِش بيِرْمي أيّ بِلاسْتِك في المُحيطات؟

أسئلة المناقشة Discussion Questions

٤. أيْه رأْيَك في الاكْتِشاف ده؟

٥. المحلّات في بلدك بتِدّي كِياس بِلاسْتِك؟

٦. بتِعْمِل أيّ حاجة علشان تِساعِد البيئة؟

٧. تِفْتِكِر البيئة مسْؤوليةْ النّاس وَلّا الحُكومة وَلّا الاتْنينْ؟

٨. تِفْتِكِر مُمْكِن نِعيش مِن غيرْ بِلاسْتِك؟

Expressions and Structures تعبيرات و تراكيب

Try to remember the Arabic expressions and structures from the article. Each English translation is followed by four choices, only one of which is correct. Refer back to the article to check your answers.

1. **hard to recycle**

   صعْب علشان يِدوّر

   صعْب التّدْوير

   صعْب يِتْعاد تدْويرُه

   يِتْعاد تدْويرُه صعْب

2. **plastic that is dumped in...**

   كِمّيةْ البِلاسْتِك اللي بِترِمي في

   كِمّيةْ البِلاسْتِك اللي بِتِتْرْمي في

   كِمّيةْ البِلاسْتِك المرْمي في

   كِمّيةْ البِلاسْتِك اللي بيِتْرْمي في

3. **only once**

   المرّة الوَحْدة بسّ

   واحْدة مرّة بسّ

   واحِد مرّة بسّ

   مرّة واحْدة بسّ

4. **300 million tons**

   تُلْتُميةْ مِلْيوْن طِنّ

   تُلْتُميةْ مِلْيوْنات طِنّ

   تُلْتُميةْ مِلْيوْنات أطْنان

   تُلْتُميةْ مِلْيوْن مِن الأطْنان

Answer Key and Translations

الإجابات و الترجمات

Key Word Answers

to discover اِكْتَشَف • discovery اِكْتِشاف • landfill مقْلب زِبالة • ocean مُحيط • to be thrown; be dumped اِترْمى • team فريق • to produce أنْتج • research, study بَحْث • to control اِتْحكّم • amount كِمّيّة

Translation of the Article

1. **Discovery: New Bacteria Eats Plastic**
2. Researchers have discovered a new type of bacteria that eats a type of plastic called polyurethane.
3. This type is hard to recycle.
4. Some scientists say that this discovery might reduce the amount of plastic {that is} dumped in landfills and oceans.
5. A team from a research center in Germany found a type of bacteria in an area that had large amounts of plastic in it.
6. The team found that the bacteria produce enzymes that break down polyurethane.
7. The German study says that scientists can easily control these bacteria and produce them for industrial use.
8. However, some researchers say that we need more research before we put these bacteria in natural environments.
9. Humans {the human} produces about 300 million tons of plastic every year.
10. Around half of this amount is used only once, and around eight million tons get dumped in oceans.

Phonemic Transcription of the Article

1. *iktišāf: baktīriya g(i)dīda bitākul ilbilástik*
2. *fī baɧisīn iktášafu baktīriya g(i)dīda bitākul nō3 min ilbilástik ísmu "puliyuriŧēn".*
3. *innō3 da şa3b(ə) yit3ād tadwīru.*
4. *fī 3úlama biyʔūlu ʔinn ilʔiktišāf da múmkin yiʔállil kammíyyit ilbilástik ílli b(i)titrími fi maʔālib izzibāla w ilmuɧiţāt.*
5. *farīʔ min márkaz ʔabɧās fi ʔalmánya, láʔa nō3 ilbaktīriya da f(i) manţíʔa kān fīha kammiyyāt ḑáxma min ilbilástik.*
6. *ilfarīʔ láʔa ʔinn ilbaktīriya bitíntig inzimāt bitkássar ilpuliyuriŧēn.*

7. *ilbáɦs ilʔalmāni biyʔūl ʔinn il3úlama múmkin yitɦakkímu fi -lbaktīriya di bi-shūla wi yintigūha li-lʔistixdamāt iṣṣina3íyya.*
8. *bassə ba3ḍ ilbaɦisīn biyʔūlu ʔinnína miɦtagīn ʔabɦās ʔáktar ʔablə ma nɦúṭṭ ilbaktīriya di f(i) biʔāt ṭabi3íyya.*
9. *ilʔinsān biyíntig ɦawāli tultumīt milyōn ṭinnə bilástik kullə sána.*
10. *ɦawāli nuṣṣ ilkammíyya di b(i)tustá3mal márra wáɦda bass, wi ɦawāli tamánya milyōn ṭinnə bilástik biyitrímu fi -lmuɦiṭāt.*

Translation of the Questions

1. Who made this discovery? 2. How much plastic do humans produce every year? 3. How much plastic doesn't get dumped in the oceans? 4. What is your opinion of this discovery? 5. Do stores in your country give [out] plastic bags? 6. Do you do anything to help the environment? 7. Do you think the environment is the responsibility of people, the government or both? 8. Do you think it is possible for us {that we} to live without plastic?

Answers to Expressions and Structures

1. hard to recycle صعْب يِتْعاد تدْويرُه
2. plastic that is dumped in... كمّيةْ البِلاسْتِك اللي بِتِترْمي في
3. only once مرّة واحْدة بسّ
4. 300 million tons تُلْتُمية مِلْيوْن طِنّ

Notes

مدينة يابانية منعت الموبايل أثناء المشي

مدينة ياماتو هي أول مدينة في اليابان تمنع استعمال الموبايل أثناء المشي في الأماكن العامة. القانون ده اتطبق في أول يوليو ٢٠٢٠. اللي عايز يستعمل موبايله لازم يقف على جنب الطريق.

مفيش عقوبة للي هيخالف القانون ده، لكن الهدف إن الناس يعرفوا خطر استعمال الموبايل أثناء المشي.

واحد من المسؤولين في المدينة بيقول إن عدد الناس اللي بيستعملوا موبايلاتهم بيزيد بسرعة، و عدد الحوادث زاد معاهم.

القانون الجديد اتقدم بعد دراسة في يناير لقت إن حوالي ١٢٪ من المشاه بيستعملوا الموبايل أثناء المشي. ده بيخلي ناس كتير يخبطوا بعض و هما ماشيين، أو يقعوا أو موبايلاتهم تقع منهم.

ناس كتير أوي، كبار و صغيرين، شجعوا القانون الجديد، و ناس قليلين جدا خالفوه لحد دلوقتي.

Japanese City Bans Phone Use While Walking

Key Words الكلمات

Study the key words and their definitions.

Translations	Definitions	Key Words
________	عكْس "سمح"	منع (يِمْنع)
________	في الوَقْت اللي حاجة تانْيَة بِتحْصل فيه	أثْناء
________	اتْفعَل	اِتْطبّق (يِتْطبّق)
________	حاجة لازِم اللي يِغْلط يعْمِلْها	عُقوبة
________	ممْشيش على نِظام مُعيّن	خالِف (يِخالِف)
________	الإسْم مِن "اِسْتعْمل"	اِسْتِعْمال
________	شخْص ليه سُلْطة شرْعية	مسْؤول / مسْؤولة
________	المبْني لِلمجْهول مِن "قدِّم"	اِتْقدِّم (يِتْقدِّم)
________	النّاس اللي بِيمْشوا على رِجْلُهم في الشّارِع	المُشاه
________	ضرب	خبط (يِخْبط)
________	نِزِل لِتحْت بِسُرْعة	وِقِع (يُقع)

Now match these translations to the key words above. Check your answers in the answer key.

official • pedestrians • punishment • to ban • to be applied, be put into effect • to be introduced • to fall • to hit • to violate, break (a law) • use, utilization • while; during

The Article

المقالة

1 مدينة يابانية منعِت الموبايْل أثْناء المشْي

2 مدينِةْ **ياماتوْ** هِيَّ أوِّل مدينة في اليابان تِمْنع اِسْتِعْمال الموبايْل أثْناء المشْي في الأماكِن العامّة.

3 القانون ده اِتْطبّق في أوِّل يولْيو عِشْرين عِشْرين.

4 اللي عايِز يِسْتعْمِل موبايْلُه لازِم يُقف على جنْب الطّريق.

5 مفيش عُقوبة لِللي هَيْخالِف القانون ده، لكِن الهدف إنّ النّاس يِعْرفوا خطر اِسْتِعْمال الموبايْل أثْناء المشْي.

6 واحِد مِن المسْؤولين في المدينة بِيْقول إنّ عدد النّاس اللي بِيِسْتعْمِلوا موبايْلاتْهُم بِيْزيد بِسُرْعة، و عدد الحَوادِث زاد معاهُم.

7 القانون الجِديد اِتْقدِّم بعْد دِراسة في يَنايِر لقت إنّ حَوالي اِتْناشر في المية مِن المُشاهْ بِيِسْتعْمِلوا الموبايْل أثْناء المشْي.

8 ده بِيْخلّي ناس كِتير يِخْبطوا بعْض و هُمّا ماشْيين، أَوْ يُقعوا أَوْ موبايْلاتْهُم تُقع مِنْهُم.

9 ناس كِتير أوي، كُبار و صُغيرّين، شجّعوا القانون الجِديد، و ناس قُليِّلين جِدّاً خالْفوه لِحدّ دِلْوَقْتي.

Comprehension Questions أسئلة الفهم

١. أيْه عُقوبة اللي يِخالِف القانون ده؟

٢. فيه مُدُن تانْيَة في اليابان طبّقِت القانون ده قبْل مدينِةْ **ياماتوْ**؟

٣. مُعْظم النّاس في المدينة بِيْخالْفوا القانون؟

Discussion Questions أسئلة المناقشة

٤. أيْه رأْيَك في القانون ده؟ تِفْتِكِر المفْروض يِتْطبّق في مدينْتك؟

٥. أيْه أغْرب قانون سمعْت عنُّه؟

٦. بِتِسْتعْمِل موبايْلك وَقْت قدّ أيْه في اليوْم؟

٧. تِقْدر تِعيش شهْر مِن غيْر موبايْلك؟ ليْه؟

٨. أيْه أكْتر حاجة بِتْحِبّها/مبِتْحِبّهاش في مدينْتك؟

Expressions and Structures تعبيرات و تراكيب

Try to remember the Arabic expressions and structures from the article. Each English translation is followed by four choices, only one of which is correct. Refer back to the article to check your answers.

1. **on July 1**

في أوِّل يولْيو	في واحِد مِن يولْيو
على يولْيو أوِّل	يولْيو واحِد

2. **while (they are) walking**

و يمْشوا	أثْناء هُمّا ماشْيين
أثْناء مشْي	و هُمّا ماشْيين

3. **the number of people who...**

ناس عديد اللي	عدد النّاس اللي
عديد النّاس اللي	العدد مِن النّاس اللي

4. **very few people**

كِتير قُلَيِّلين مِن النّاس	ناس قُلَيِّلين خلاص
ناس كِتير جِدّاً	ناس قُلَيِّلين جِدّاً

Answer Key and Translations الإجابات و الترجمات

Key Word Answers

to ban منع • while; during أثْناء • to be applied, be put into effect اِتْطبّق • punishment عُقوبة • to violate, break (a law) خالِف • use, utilization اِسْتِعْمال • official مسْؤول • to be introduced اِتْقدِّم • pedestrians المُشاه • to hit خبط • to fall وِقِع

Translation of the Article

1. **Japanese City Bans Phone Use While Walking**
2. Yamato City {it, she} is the first city in Japan to ban using phones while walking in public places.
3. This law was put into effect on July 1, 2020.
4. Whoever wants to use their phone has to step to the side of the road.
5. There is no punishment for those who violate this law, but the goal is that people know the danger of using phones while walking.
6. One city official {one of the officials in the city} says that the number of people who use their phones is increasing rapidly, and the number of accidents has increased as a result {with them [people who use their phones]}.
7. The new law was introduced after a study in January [that] found that around 12% of pedestrians use their phones while walking.
8. This causes many people to hit each other while walking, fall, or drop their phones {their phones fall from them}.
9. So many people, old and young, have supported the new law, and very few people have violated it so far.

Phonemic Transcription of the Article

1. *madīna yabaníyya mána3it ilmubāyl ʔasnāʔ ilmášy*
2. *madīnit yamatō híyya ʔáwwil madīna fi -lyabān tímna3 isti3māl ilmubāyl ʔasnāʔ ilmášy(ə) fi -lʔamākin il3ámma.*
3. *ilqanūn da (i)tṭábbaʔ fi ʔáwwil yúlyu 3išrīn 3išrīn.*
4. *ílli 3āyiz yistá3mil mubāylu lāzim yúʔaf 3ála gamb iṭṭarīʔ.*

5. *ma-fīš 3uqūba lí-lli hayxālif ilqanūn da, lākin ilhádaf ʔinn innās yi3ráfu xátar isti3māl ilmubāyl ʔasnāʔ ilmášy.*
6. *wāħid min ilmasʔulīn fi -lmadīna biyʔūl ʔinnə 3ádad innās ílli b(i)yista3mílu mubayláthum biyzīd bi-súr3a, wi 3ádad ilħawādis zād ma3āhum.*
7. *ilqanūn ilgidīd itʔáddim ba3də dirāsa fi yanāyir láʔit ʔinnə ħawāli (i)tnāšar fi -lmíyya min ilmušāh biyista3mílu -lmubāyl ʔasnāʔ ilmášy.*
8. *da biyxálli nās kitīr yixbátu ba3d(ə) w(i) húmma mašyīn, ʔaw yúʔa3u ʔaw mubayláthum túʔa3 mínhum.*
9. *nās kitīr ʔáwi, kubār wi ṣuɣayyarīn, šaggá3u -lqanūn ilgidīd, wi nās ʔulayyilīn gíddan xalfū li-ħáddə dilwáʔti.*

Translation of the Questions

1. What is the punishment for breaking this law? 2. Are there other cities in Japan that implemented this law before Yamato? 3. Do many people in the city break the this law? 4. What is your opinion of this law? Do you think it should be implemented in your town? 5. What is the strangest law you have heard of? 6. How much {time} do you use your phone per day? 7. Could you go {live} a month wihout your phone? Why (not)? 8. What do you like most/least about your town?

Answers to Expressions and Structures

1. on July 1 في أوِّل يولْيو
2. while (they are) walking و هُمّا ماشْيين
3. the number of people who... عدد النّاس اللي
4. very few people ناس قُلَيِّلين جِدّاً

Notes

فرنسا حولت النبيت اللي متباعش لمطهر إيد

الحكومة الفرنساوية لقت طريقة جديدة عشان تساعد صناعة النبيت. مصانع النبيت بدئت تبيع النبيت اللي متباعش للحكومة عشان الحكومة تحوله لمطهر إيد.

الحكومة ناوية تعمل مطهرات إيد و إيثانول من النبيت اللي متباعش. الإيثانول ممكن يستعمل في منتجات كتير.

الاتحاد الأوروبي وافق إنه يدفع لمصانع النبيت من ٦٥ لـ٨٨ دولار، على حسب النوع، في كل مية لتر نبيت.

مبيعات النبيت في فرنسا قلت بعد ما أمريكا زودت ضريبة ٢٥٪ في المية على أي نبيت مستورد في أكتوبر ٢٠١٩. و بعد كده، المبيعات قلت أكتر و أكتر عشان البارات و المطاعم قفلوا بسبب كورونا.

فيه مصنع أسباني أخد المبادرة دي قبل فرنسا، و إيطاليا ناوية تعمل زي فرنسا.

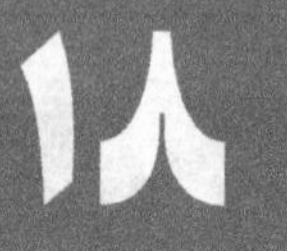

France Turns Unsold Wine Into Hand Sanitizer

Key Words

الكلمات

Study the key words and their definitions.

Translations	Definitions	Key Words
____________	أُسْلوب	طريقة (طُرُق)
____________	مشْروب كُحولي معْمول مِن العِنب	نِبيت
____________	غيرّ حدّ أَوْ حاجة	حَوِّل (يِحَوِّل)
____________	حاجة بِتِتْعمِل عشان تِتْباع	مُنْتج
____________	عكْس "رفض"	وافِق (يوافِق)
____________	خلّى حاجة تِبْقى أكْتر	زوِّد (يِزوِّد)
____________	فِلوس الحُكومة بِتاخِدْها عشان تِساعِد البلد	ضريبة (ضرايِب)
____________	خطْوَة لِحلّ مُشْكِلة	مُبادْرة

Now match these translations to the key words above. Check your answers in the answer key.

initiative • product • tax • to agree • to increase •
to turn (something) • way, method • wine

The Article

المقالة

1 فرنْسا حوّلِت النِّبيت اللي متْباعْش لِمُطهِّر إيد

2 الحُكومة الفرنْساوية لقِت طريقة جِديدة عشان تِساعِد صِناعةْ النِّبيت.

3 مصانع النِّبيت بدئِت تِبيع النِّبيت اللي متْباعْش لِلحُكومة عشان الحُكومة تِحوِّلُه لِمُطهِّر إيد.

4 الحُكومة ناوْيَة تِعْمِل مُطهِّرات إيد و إيثانول مِن النِّبيت اللي متْباعْش.

5 الإيثانول مُمْكِن يُسْتعْمل في مُنْتجات كِتير.

6 الاتِّحاد الأوروبيّ وافِق إنُّه يِدْفع لِمصانع النِّبيت مِن خمْسة و ستّين لِتمانْيَة و تمانين دولار، على حسب النّوْع، في كُلّ مية لِترْ نبيت.

7 مبيعات النِّبيت في فرنْسا قلِّت بعْد ما أمْريكا زوِّدت ضريبة خمْسة و عِشْرين في المية على أيّ نِبيت مُسْتوْرد في أُكْتوْبِر ألفيْن و تِسعْتاشر.

8 و بعْد كِده، المبيعات قلِّت أكْتر و أكْتر عشان البارات و المطاعِم قفلوا بِسبب كورونا.

9 فيه مصْنع أسْباني أخد المُبادْرة دي قبْل فرنْسا، و إيطالْيا ناوْيَة تِعْمِل زيّ فرنْسا.

أسئلة الفهم Comprehension Questions

١. ليْه مبيعات النِّبيت قلِّت في فرنْسا؟

٢. الاتِّحاد الأُروبيّ هَيِشْترِي الـ١٠٠ لِترْ نِبيت بِكام؟

٣. هل فرنْسا هِيَّ أوِّل بلد تاخِد المُبادْرة دي؟

أسئلة المناقشة Discussion Questions

٤. أيْه رأْيَك في المُبادْرة دي؟

٥. لَوْ لازِم تِعيش في فرنْسا أَوْ إيطالْيا أَوْ أسْبانْيا، هتِخْتار أنْهي بلد و ليْه؟

٦. بِتْحِبّ الأكْل الفرنْساوي؟

٧. بِتِسْتعْمِل مُطهِّر إيد وَلّا لأ؟ لَوْ آه، كُلّ قدّ أيْه؟

٨. أيْه أكْتر مشْروب بِتْحِبّ تِشْربُه؟

Expressions and Structures تعبيرات و تراكيب

Try to remember the Arabic expressions and structures from the article. Each English translation is followed by four choices, only one of which is correct. Refer back to the article to check your answers.

1. **wine that was not sold**

النِّبيت متْباعْش | النِّبيت اللي متْباعْش

نِبيت مِش متْبوع | نِبيت اللي مِش اتْباع

2. **[he, it] agreed to pay**

وافْقة إنُّها يِدْفع | وافِق عشان يِدْفع

مُوَفّق يِدْفع | وافِق إنُّه يِدْفع

3. **wine sales have decreased**

مبيعات النِّبيت قلِّت | المبيعات نِبيت قلِّت

مبيع النِّبيت قلّ | المبيع النِّبيت قلّ

4. ***(conjunction)* after**

بعْد كِده | بعْد إنّ

بعْد ما | بعْد اللي

Answer Key and Translations

الإجابات و الترجمات

Key Word Answers

way, method طريقة • wine نِبيت • to turn حَوِّل • product مُنْتَج • to agree وافِق • to increase زوِّد • tax ضريبة • initiative مُبادْرة

Translation of the Article

1. **France Turns Unsold Wine Into Hand Sanitizer**
2. The French government has found a new way to help the wine industry.
3. Winemakers have started to sell unsold wine {that was not sold} to the government so that the government turns it into a hand sanitizer.
4. The government is planning to make hand sanitizers and ethanol out of the unsold wine.
5. Ethanol can be used in many products.
6. The European Union agreed to pay winemakers $65-$88, depending on the type, for every 100 liters of wine.
7. Sales of wine in France have decreased after the US added a 25% tax on any imported wine in October 2019.
8. And after that, sales have decreased even more because bars and restaurants closed because of the coronavirus [pandemic].
9. A Spanish winemaker took this initiative before France, and Italy is planning to do like France.

Phonemic Transcription of the Article

1. *faránsa ɧawwálit innibīt ílli ma-tbá3š(ə) li-muţáhhir ʔīd*
2. *ilɧukūma -lfaransawíyya láʔit ţarīʔa g(i)dīda 3ašān tisā3id şinā3it innibīt.*
3. *maşāni3 innibīt bádaʔit tibī3 innibīt ílli ma-tbá3šə li-lɧukūma 3ašān ilɧukūma tiɧawwílu li-muţáhhir ʔīd.*
4. *ilɧukūma náwya tí3mil muţahhirāt ʔīd wi ʔiŧanūl min innibīt ílli ma-tbá3š.*
5. *ilʔiŧanūl múmkin yustá3mal fi muntagāt kitīr.*

6. *ilʔittiḫād ilʔurúbbi wāfiʔ ʔínnu yídfa3 li-maṣāni3 innibīt min xámsa w sittīn li-tamánya w tamanīn dulār, 3ála ḫásab innō3, fi kullə mīt li-tr(ə) nibīt.*
7. *mabi3āt innibīt fi faránsa ʔállit ba3də ma ʔamrīka zawwídit ḍarība xámsa wi 3išrīn fi -lmíyya 3ála ʔayyə nibīt mustáwrad fi ʔuktōbir ʔalfēn wi tisa3tāšar.*
8. *wi ba3də kída, ilmabi3āt ʔállit ʔáktar wi ʔáktar 3ašān ilbarāt w ilmaṭā3im ʔáfalu bi-sábab kurōna.*
9. *fī máṣna3 ʔasbāni ʔáxad ilmubádra di ʔablə faránsa, w iṭálya náwya tí3mil zayyə faránsa.*

Translation of the Questions

1. Why have wine sales fallen in France? 2. How much will the European Union buy a 100 liters of wine for? 3. Was France the first country to take this initiative? 4. What is your opinion of this initiative? 5. If you had to live in France, Italy, or Spain, which country would you choose and why? 6. Do you like French food? 7. Do you use hand sanitizer? If so, how often? 8. What is your favorite beverage to drink?

Answers to Expressions and Structures

1. wine that was not sold النّبيت اللي متْباعْش
2. agreed to pay وافِق إنُّه يِدْفع
3. wine sales have decreased مبيعات النّبيت قلّت
4. *(conjunction)* after بعْد ما

Notes

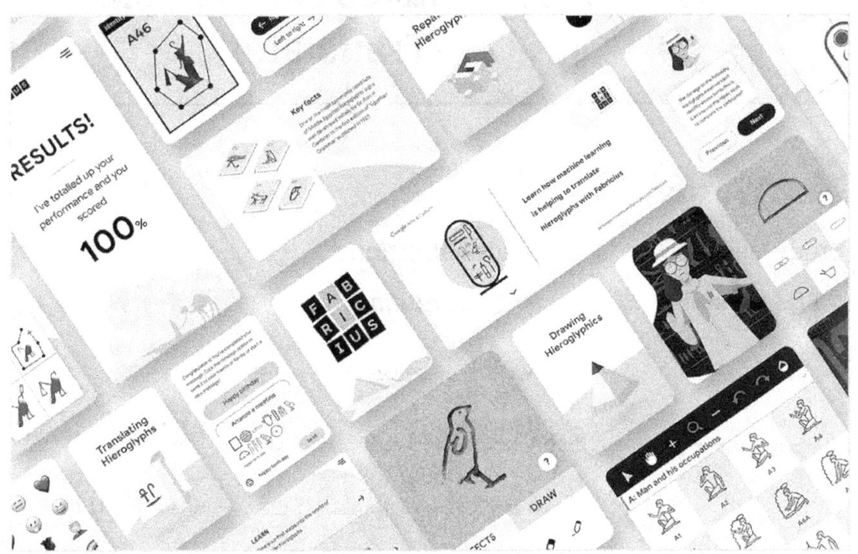

جوجل عملت تطبيق بيترجم الهيروغليفي

اللغة المصرية القديمة أو اللغة الهيروغليفية هي واحدة من اللغات الصعبة. بس جوجل احتفلت بذكرى اكتشاف حجر رشيد بإنهم عملوا تطبيق فابريشيوس اللي هيساعد العلما إنهم يقروا اللغة الهيروغليفية.

التطبيق ده برضه هيساعد ناس أكتر إنهم يعرفوا أكتر عن الحضارة المصرية بطريقة سهلة. التطبيق موجود على الموقع المجاني جوجل آرتس آند كالتشر (جوجل للفنون و الثقافة).

التطبيق الجديد بيترجم الهيروغليفي للإنجليزي و العربي، و المعلومات دي ممكن تتشاف بتكنولوچيا الواقع الافتراضي.

مدير برنامج جوجل آرتس آند كالتشر تشانس كوجينور قال إن التطبيق فيه تلات أقسام: التعلم و اللعب و الشغل الأكاديمي. و قال إن أقسام التعلم و اللعب بساط و ممتعين في حين إن القسم الأكاديمي بيساعد الباحثين و العلما.

١٩ Google Makes Hieroglyphics Translator

Key Words

الكلمات

Study the key words and their definitions.

Translations	Definitions	Key Words
______	نِظام تَواصُل بينْ مجْموعة كِبيرة مِن النّاس	لُغَة
______	عمل حاجة مُميّزة عشان مُناسْبة مُعيّنة	اِحْتفل (يِحْتِفِل)
______	وَقْت كُلّ سنة بِيْفكّر بِحاجة حصلِت فيه زيّ الوَقْت ده قبْل كِده	ذِكْرى (ذِكْرَيات)
______	حاجة اِتْعرفِت لأِوِّل مرّة	اِكْتِشاف
______	برْنامِج كُمْپْيوتر	تطْبيق
______	نقل كلام للُغة تانْيَة	ترْجِم (يترْجِم)
______	المبْني لِلمجْهول مِن "شاف"	اِتْشاف (يِتْشاف)
______	جُزْء	قِسْم (أقْسام)
______	سهْل	بسيط (بُساط)
______	بِيْخلّيك تِنْبِسِط؛ تِحِسّ بمِتْعة	مُمتِع

Now match these translations to the key words above. Check your answers in the answer key.

anniversary • app • discovery • enjoyable, fun • language • section • simple • to be seen • to celebrate • to translate

The Article

المقالة

1 **جوجل** عملِت تطْبيق بيِترْجِم الهيروغْليفي

2 اللُّغة المصْرية القديمة أَوْ اللُّغة الهيروغْليفية هِيَّ واحْدة مِن اللُّغات الصّعْبة.

3 بسّ **جوجل** اِحْتفلِت بِذِكْرى اِكْتِشاف حجر رشيد بِإِنُّهُمْ عملوا تطْبيق **فابريشيوس** اللي هَيْساعِد العُلما إِنُّهُمْ يِقْروا اللُّغة الهيروغْليفية.

4 التّطْبيق ده برْضُه هَيْساعِد ناس أكْتر إِنُّهُمْ يِعْرفوا أكْتر عن الحضارة المصْرية بِطريقة سهْلة.

5 التّطْبيق مَوْجود على المَوْقِع المجّاني **جوجل آرْتْس آنْد كالتْشر** (جوجل لِلفُنون و الثّقافة.)

6 التّطْبيق الجديد بِيْترْجِم الهيروغْليفي لِلإِنْجِليزي و العربي، و المعْلومات دي مُمْكِن تِتْشاف بِتِكْنولوچْيا الواقِع الافْتِراضي.

7 مُدير برْنامِج **جوجل آرْتْس آنْد كالتْشر تْشانْس كوجينَوْر** قال إِنّ التّطْبيق فيه تلات أَقْسام: التّعلُّم و اللِّعْب و الشُّغْل الأكاديمي.

8 و قال إِنّ أَقْسام التّعلُّم و اللِّعْب بُساط و مُمْتِعين في حين إِنّ القِسْم الأكاديمي بِيْساعِد الباحِثين و العُلما.

أسئلة الفهم Comprehension Questions

١. **جوجل** اِحْتفلت بِذِكْرى اِكْتِشاف حجر رشيد إزّاي؟

٢. مَوْقِع **جوجل آرْتْس آنْد كالتْشر** بِكام؟

٣. فيه كام قِسْم في التّطْبيق الجِديد؟

أسئلة المناقشة Discussion Questions

٤. أيْه رأْيَك في التّطْبيق الجِديد؟ هتِسْتعْمِلُه؟

٥. لَوْ عملْت تطْبيق، هَيِعْمِل أيْه؟

٦. أيْه أكْتر التّطْبيقات اللي بِتِسْتعْمِلْها؟

٧. لُغتك سهْلة وَلّا صعْبة؟ تِفْتِكِر أيْه هِيَّ أصْعب لُغة في العالم؟

٨. أيْه المهارات اللي إنْتَ عايِز تِتْعلِّمْها؟

Expressions and Structures تعبيرات و تراكيب

Try to remember the Arabic expressions and structures from the article. Each English translation is followed by four choices, only one of which is correct. Refer back to the article to check your answers.

1. **the ancient Egyptian language**

لُغة قديمة لِلمصْريّين — اللُّغة المصْرية القديمة

اللُّغة المصْريّين القُدما — اللُّغة قديمة مصْرية

2. **in an easy way**

بِالطّريق السّهْلي — بِطريقة السّهْلة

بِطريقة سهْلة — بِسْهولةْ الطّريقة

3. **this information can be viewed**

المعْلومة دي مُمْكِنة يِتْشوف — المعْلومات دي مُمْكِن تِشوف

المعْلوم ده مُمْكِن يِشاف — المعْلومات دي مُمْكِن تِتْشاف

4. **whereas**

فينْ زيّ — فيه حين عشان

في حين إنّ — بِحين

Answer Key and Translations

الإجابات و الترجمات

Key Word Answers

language لُغة • to celebrate اِحْتفل • anniversary ذِكْرى • discovery اِكْتِشاف • app تطْبيق • to translate ترْجِم • to be seen اِتْشاف • section قِسْم • simple بسيط • enjoyable, fun مُمتع

Translation of the Article

1. **Google Makes Hieroglyphics Translator**
2. The Ancient Egyptian Language, or Hieroglyphs, {she} is a difficult language {one of the difficult languages}.
3. But Google celebrated the anniversary of the Rosetta Stone's discovery by making the app Fabricius, which will help scientists read Hieroglyphs.
4. This app will also help more people know more about Egyptian civilization in an easy way.
5. The app is on the free website Google Arts & Culture.
6. The new app translates Hieroglyphs to English and Arabic, and this information can be viewed using virtual reality technology.
7. Director of the Google Arts and Culture program, Chance Coughenour, said that the application consists of three sections, learning, playing, and academic work.
8. He also said that the sections for learning and playing are simple and fun, whereas the academic section helps researchers and scientists.

Phonemic Transcription of the Article

1. *[Google] 3ámalit taṭbīʔ biytárgim ilhiruɣlīfi*
2. *illúɣa (i)lmaṣríyya ilʔadīma, ʔaw illúɣa (i)lhiruɣlifíyya, híyya wáђda min illuɣāt iṣṣá3ba.*
3. *bassə [Google] iђtáfalit bi-zíkra iktišāf ђágar rašīd bi-ʔinnúhum 3ámalu taṭbīʔ [Fabricius] ílli haysā3id il3úlama ʔinnúhum yíʔru -llúɣa (i)lhiruɣlifíyya.*
4. *ittaṭbīʔ da bárḍu haysā3id nās ʔáktar ʔinnúhum yi3ráfu ʔáktar 3an ilђaḍāra ilmaṣríyya bi-ṭarīʔa sáhla.*

5. *ittaṭbīʔ mawgūd 3ála -lmáwqi3 ilmaggāni [Google Arts and Culture] ([Google] li-lfunūn w issaqāfa).*
6. *ittaṭbīʔ ilgidīd biytárgim ilhiruɣlīfi li-lʔingilīzi w il3árabi, w ilma3lumāt di múmkin titšāf bi-tiknulúžya -lwáqi3 ilʔiftirāḍi.*
7. *mudīri barnāmig [Google Arts and Culture] [Chance Coughenour] ʔāl ʔinn ittaṭbīʔ fī tálat ʔaqsām: itta3állum w illí3b w iššúɣl ilʔakadīmi.*
8. *wi ʔāl ʔinnə ʔaqsām itta3állum w illí3b busāṭ wi mumti3īn fi ḥīn ʔinn ilqísm ilʔakadīmi biysā3id ilbaḥisīn w il3úlama.*

Translation of the Questions

1. How did Google celebrate the anniversary of the discovery of the Rosetta Stone? 2. How much does the Google Arts and Culture website cost? 3. How many sections are there in the new app? 4. What do you think about the new app? Will you use it? 5. If you made an app, what would it do? 6. What app do you use most? 7. Is your language easy or difficult? What do you think is the most difficult language in the world? 8. What skills would you like to learn?

Answers to Expressions and Structures

1. the ancient Egyptian language اللُّغة المصْرية القديمة
2. in an easy way بِطريقة سهْلة
3. this information can be viewed المعْلومات دي مُمْكِن تِتْشاف
4. whereas في حين إنّ

Notes

الحشرات قلت ٢٧٪ في ٣٠ سنة

في آخر ٣٠ سنة، الحشرات قلت ٢٧٪ في المية، طبقا للمجلة العلمية ساينس.

الحشرات بتقل بمعدل أقل حاجة بسيطة من ١٪ في السنة.

رقم الحشرات بيقل في المناطق الزراعية و المدن و الضواحي أكتر من أي أماكن تاني، بالذات في أجزاء من شمال أمريكا و أوروبا.

بس في حين إن الحشرات الأرضية بتقل، الحشرات المائية، زي الناموس، بتزيد بمعدل ١٪ في السنة. ده أسرع من المعدل اللي الحشرات الأرضية بتقل بيه، بس الحشرات المائية قليلة جدا بالمقارنة بكل الحشرات اللي في العالم.

بس العلما بيقولوا إن زيادة الحشرات المائية علامة كويسة، لإن ده غالبا معناه إن الأنهار بقت أنضف.

٢٠

Insects Decrease by 27% in 30 Years

Study the key words and their definitions.

Translations	Definitions	Key Words
______	كائِن صُغيّر عنْدُه سِتّ رُجول	حشرة
______	نِسْبة	مُعدّل
______	ليه عِلاقة بِالأرْض	أرْضي
______	ليه عِلاقة بِالمايّة	مائي
______	مكان على طرف مدينة	ضاحْيَة (ضَواحي)
______	ليه علاقة بِالزِّراعة	زِراعي
______	بِالنِّسْبة لِـ	بِالمُقارْنة بِـ
______	طريق مايّة حِلْوة طَويل زيّ النّيل	نهر (أنْهار)
______	الرّقم اللي خلّى حاجة أكْتر	زِيادة
______	إشارة	علامة
______	بدأ يكون مُخْتلِف عن الأوّل	بقى (يِبْقى)

Now match these translations to the key words above. Check your answers in the answer key.

agricultural • aquatic • average, rate • in comparison with • increase • insect • river • sign • suburb • terrestrial • to become

المقالة The Article

1 الحشرات قلِّت سبْعة و عِشْرين في المية في تلاتين سنة

2 في آخِر تلاتين سنة، الحشرات قلِّت سبْعة و عِشْرين في المية، طِبْقاً لِلمجلّة العِلْمية **سايِنْس**.

3 الحشرات بِتْقِلّ بمِعُدّل أقلّ حاجة بسيطة مِن واحِد في المية في السّنة.

4 رقِم الحشرات بِيْقِلّ في المناطِق الزِّراعية و المُدُن و الضَواحي أكْتر مِن أيّ أماكِن تاني، بِالذّات في أجْزاء مِن شمال أمْريكا و أوروبّا.

5 بسّ في حين إنّ الحشرات الأرْضية بِتْقِلّ، الحشرات المائية، زيّ النّاموس، بِتْزيد بمِعُدّل واحِد في المية في السّنة.

6 ده أسْرع مِن المعُدّل اللي الحشرات الأرْضية بِتْقِلّ بيه، بسّ الحشرات المائية قُلَيِّلة جِدّاً بِالمُقارْنة بِكُلّ الحشرات اللي في العالم.

7 بسّ العُلما بِيْقولوا إنّ زِيادِةْ الحشرات المائية علامة كُوَيِّسة، لإِنّ ده غالِباً معْناه إنّ الأنْهار بقِت أنْضف.

أسئلة الفهم Comprehension Questions

١. كُلّ أنْواع الحشرات في العالَم بتْقِلّ؟

٢. زِيادِةْ الحشرات المائية علامة على أيْه؟

٣. أيْه أكْتر أماكِن الحشرات بتْقِلّ فيها؟

أسئلة المناقشة Discussion Questions

٤. أيْه رأْيَك الخبر ده؟

٥. بتْحِبّ أيّ حشرة؟ لَوْ آه، أيْه هِيَّ؟ لَوْ لأة، لأة ليْه؟

٦. الحشرات فيها بِروتين كِتير. مُمْكِن تجرّب تاكْلْها؟

٧. تِفْتِكِر ليْه الحشرات بتْقِلّ كِتير في المناطِق الزِّراعية و المُدُن و الضَّواحي؟

٨. تِفْتِكِر المفْروض كُلّ النّاموس يمِوت؟

Expressions and Structures تعبيرات و تراكيب

Try to remember the Arabic expressions and structures from the article. Each English translation is followed by four choices, only one of which is correct. Refer back to the article to check your answers.

1. **in the last thirty years**

   في آخِر تلاتين سنة

   في الآخِر تلاتين سنة

   في التّلاتين سِنين الأخيرة

   في تلاتين مِن السّنة الأخيرة

2. **according to**

   طبْعاً لِـ

   مُعدّل بِـ

   بِالمُقارْنة بِـ

   طِبْقاً لِـ

3. **a bit less**

   أقلّ الحاجة القُلَيِّلة

   أكْتر حاجة بسيطة

   أقلّ حاجة بسيطة

   حاجة قُلَيِّلة أكْتر

4. **most likely, probably**

   معْناه إنّ

   غالِباً

   في أكْبار الأجْزاء

   طِبْقاً

Answer Key and Translations

الإجابات و الترجمات

Key Word Answers

insect حشرة • average, rate مُعدّل • terrestrial أرْضي • aquatic مائي • suburb ضاحْيَة • agricultural زِراعي • in comparison with بِالمُقارْنة بِ • river نهر • increase زِيادة • sign علامة • to become بقى

Translation of the Article

1. **Insects Decrease by 27% in 30 Years**
2. In the last 30 years, insects have decreased [in number] by 27%, according to the scientific journal Science.
3. Insects are decreasing at an average of just a bit less than 1% per year {in the year}.
4. The number of insects is decreasing in agricultural lands {regions}, cities, and suburbs more than any other place{s}, especially in parts of North America and Europe.
5. But whereas terrestrial insects are decreasing, aquatic insects, like mosquitoes, are increasing at {a rate of} 1% per year.
6. This is faster than the rate at which terrestrial insects are decreasing, but aquatic insects are too few in comparison with all of the insects in the world.
7. But scientists say that the increase of aquatic insects is a good sign because this most likely means {its meaning [is]} that rivers have become cleaner.

Phonemic Transcription of the Article

1. *ilḫašarāt ʔállit sáb3a w 3išrīn fi -lmíyya fi talatīn sána*
2. *fi ʔāxir talatīn sána, ilḫašarāt ʔállit sáb3a w(i) 3išrīn fi -lmíyya, ṭibʔqan li-lmagálla -l3ilmíyya [Science].*
3. *ilḫašarāt bitʔíll(ə) b(i)-mu3áddal ʔaʔállə ḫāga basīṭa min wāḫid fi -lmíyya fi -ssána.*
4. *ráqam ilḫašarāt biyʔíll(ə) fi -lmanāṭiʔ izzira3íyya w ilmúdun w ilḍawāḫi ʔáktar min ʔayyə ʔamākin tāni, bi-zzāt fi ʔagzāʔ min šamāl ʔamrīka wi ʔurúbba.*
5. *bass(ə) fi ḫīn ʔinn ilḫašarāt ilʔaraḍíyya bitʔíll, ilḫašarāt ilmaʔíyya, zayy innamūs, bitzīd bi-mu3áddal wāḫid fi -lmíyya fi -ssána.*

6. *da ʔásra3 min ilmu3áddal ílli -lħašarāt ilʔarḍíyya bitʔíllə bī, bass ilħašarāt ilmaʔíyya ʔulayyíla gíddan bi-lmuqárna bikúll ilħašarāt ílli fi -l3ālam.*
7. *báss il3úlama biyʔūlu ʔinnə ziyādit ilħašarāt ilmaʔíyya 3alāma k(u)wayyísa, li-ʔinnə da ɣalíban ma3nā ʔinn ilʔanhār báʔit ʔánḍaf.*

Translation of the Questions

1. Are all species of insects in the world decreasing? 2. What is the increase of aquatic insects a sign of? 3. What are the places where insects are decreasing the most? 4. What is your opinion of this news? 5. Do you like any insect? If so, which one? If not, why not? 6. Insects have a lot of protein {in them}. Would you try {eating} them? 7. Why do you think insects are decreasing in agricultural areas, cities, and suburbs? 8. Do you think all mosquitoes should die?

Answers to Expressions and Structures

1. in the last thirty years في آخِر تلاتين سنة
2. according to طِبْقاً لِـ
3. a bit less أقلّ حاجة بسيطة
4. most likely, probably غالِباً

Notes

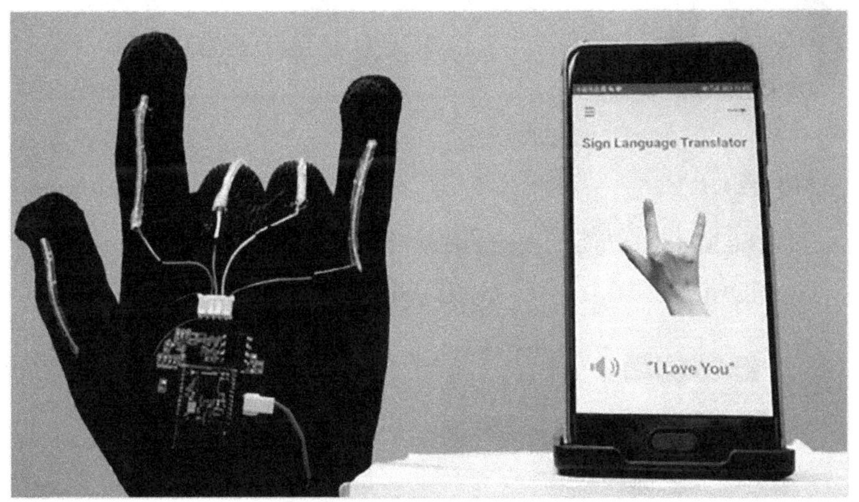

جوانتي بيترجم لغة الإشارة لكلام

فيه باحثين من جامعة كاليفورنيا، لوس أنچلوس عملوا جوانتي بيقدر يترجم لغة الإشارة الأمريكية (ASL) لإنجليزي.

الجوانتي بيعرف يقرا لغة الإشارة و بينقلها لتطبيق على الموبايل. التطبيق بعد كده بيترجم الإشارات لكلمات و بيقولها بالإنجليزي.

الهدف من الجوانتي ده إن الناس الطرش يقدروا يتكلموا مع أي حد من غير مترجم.

الجوانتي بيترجم صح بنسبة ٩٩٪ في المية.

الجوانتي كمان بيقرا تعبيرات الوش.

الباحثين اللي عملوا الجوانتي بيقولوا إن التكنولوچيات التانية اللي بتترجم لغة الإشارة الأمريكية تقيلة و مش مريحة، لكن الجوانتي خفيف و مريح.

منظمة الصحة العالمية بتقول إن فيه ٤٦٦ مليون أطرش في العالم، و نسبة كبيرة منهم بيعتمدوا على لغة الإشارة.

Gloves Translate Sign Language Into Speech

Key Words الكلمات

Study the key words and their definitions.

Translations	Definitions	Key Words
____________	حاجة بتِتْلبِس في الإيد	جُوانتي (جُوانتِيّات)
____________	مِش بيِعْرف يِسْمع	أطْرش / طرْشا (طُرْش)
____________	طريقة لِلتّواصُل بِلُغة الجسد عشان الطُّرْش	لُغةْ الإشارة
____________	حركات الوِشّ اللي بِتِحْصل بِسبب المشاعِر	تعْبيرات الوِشّ
____________	رقم في كُلّ مية	نِسْبة (نِسب)
____________	عكْس "تِقيل"	خفيف (خُفاف)
____________	بِيْسبِّب راحة	مُريح
____________	اِحْتاج حاجة بِشكْل أساسي	اِعْتمد (يِعْتِمِد) على

Now match these translations to the key words above. Check your answers in the answer key.

comfortable, cozy • deaf • facial expressions • light(weight) • pair of gloves • percentage, ratio • sign language • to depend on

The Article المقالة

1 جُوانْتي بيِتْرجِم لُغةْ الإشارة لِكلام

2 فيه باحِثين مِن جامْعةْ **كاليفورْنِيا**، **لوْس أنْچلوس** عملوا جُوانْتي بيِقْدر يِترجِم لُغِةْ الإشارة الأمْريكية (ASL) لإِنْجِليزي.

3 الجُوانْتي بيِعْرف يِقْرا لُغِةْ الإشارة و بيِنْقِلْها لِتطْبيق على الموبايْل.

4 التّطْبيق بعْد كِده بيِتْرجِم الإشارات لِكلمات و بيْقولْها بِالإِنْجِليزي.

5 الهدف مِن الجُوانْتي ده إنّ النّاس الطُّرْش يِقْدروا يِتْكلِّموا معَ أيّ حدّ مِن غيرْ مُترْجِم.

6 الجُوانْتي بيِتْرجِم صحّ بِنِسْبةْ تِسْعة و تِسْعين في المية.

7 الجُوانْتي كمان بيِقْرا تعْبيرات الوِشّ.

8 الباحِثين اللي عملوا الجُوانْتي بيْقولوا إنّ التِّكْنولوچْيات التّانْيَة اللي بِتْرجِم لُغِةْ الإشارة الأمْريكية تِقيلة و مِش مُريحة، لكِن الجُوانْتي ده خفيف و مُريح.

9 مُنظّمِةْ الصِّحّة العالمية بِتْقول إنّ فيه رُبْعمية ستّة و ستّين مِلْيوْن أطْرش في العالم، و نِسْبة كِبيرة مِنْهُم بيِعْتمِدوا على لُغِةْ الإشارة.

أسئلة الفهم Comprehension Questions

١. فيه كام أطْرش في العالم؟

٢. أيْه الهدف مِن الجُوانْتي ده؟

٣. الجُوانْتي بيِعْرف يِقْرا تعْبيرات الوِشّ؟

أسئلة المناقشة Discussion Questions

٤. أيْه رأْيَك في الجُوانْتي ده؟

٥. تِفْتِكِر دِلْوَقْتي فيه ناس طُرْش أكْتر مِن زمان؟ ليْه إنْتَ شايِف كِده؟

٦. بِتعْرف أيّ لُغةْ إشارة؟ لَوْ آه، اِتْعلمْتها إزّاي؟ لَوْ لأة، تِحِبّ تِتْعلِّم؟

٧. تِفْتِكِر العالم كُلُّه في يوْم مِن الأيّام مُمْكِن يِتْكلِّم لُغة واحْدة؟ ليْه؟

٨. بِتِسْتعْمِل أيّ تطْبيقات ترْجمة، زيّ **جوجل ترانْسْليْت**، مثلاً؟

Expressions and Structures تعبيرات و تراكيب

Try to remember the Arabic expressions and structures from the article. Each English translation is followed by four choices, only one of which is correct. Refer back to the article to check your answers.

1. **American Sign Language**

اللُّغةْ الإشارة الأمْريكية	لُغةِ إشارة أمْريكية
اللُّغةْ إشارة أمْريكية	لُغةِ الإشارة الأمْريكية

2. **the goal of these gloves**

الهدف مِن الجُوانْتي ده	الهدف الجُوانْتي دوْل
هدف الجُوانْتي ده	الهدف مِن الجُوانْتي دي

3. **[the gloves] translate correctly**

بِيْترْجِم صحيحاً	بِيْترْجِم صحّي
بِيْترْجِم صحّ	بِيْترْجِم بِشكْل الصّحّ

4. **four hundred and sixty-six**

أرْبع ميات سِتّة و سِتّين	رُبْعُمية سِتّة و سِتّين
أرْبعة مية و سِتّين سِتّة	رُبْع مية سِتّ و سِتّين

Answer Key and Translations

الإجابات و الترجمات

Key Word Answers

pair of gloves جُوانتي • deaf أطْرش • sign language لُغةْ الإشارة •
facial expressions تعْبيرات الوِشّ • percentage, ratio نِسْبة •
light(weight) خفيف • comfortable, cozy مُريح • to depend on اِعْتمد

Translation of the Article

1. **Gloves Translate Sign Language Into Speech**
2. {There are} researchers from the University of California, Los Angeles (who) have made gloves that can translate American Sign Language (ASL) to English.
3. The gloves can read sign language and transfer it to an app {on the phone}.
4. The app then translates the signs to words and says them in English.
5. The goal of these gloves is that deaf people can speak with anyone without an interpreter.
6. The gloves translate correctly 99% of the time {with a percentage of 99%}.
7. The gloves also read facial expressions.
8. The researchers who made the gloves say that other technologies that translate ASL are heavy and uncomfortable, but these gloves are lightweight and comfortable.
9. The World Health Organization says that there are 466 million deaf people in the world, and a large percentage of them depend on sign language.

Phonemic Transcription of the Article

1. *guwánti biytárgim lúɣit ilʔišāra li-kalām*
2. *fī baḫisīn min gám3it kalifúrniya, [Los Angeles] 3ámalu guwánti biyíʔdar yitárgim lúɣit ilʔišāra -lʔamrikíyya ([ASL]) li-ʔingilīzi.*
3. *ilguwánti biyí3raf yíʔra lúɣit ilʔišāra wi biyinʔílha li-taṭbīʔ 3ála -lmubāyl.*
4. *ittaṭbīʔ ba3də kída biytárgim ilʔišarāt li-kalimāt wi biyʔúlha bi-lʔingilīzi.*

5. *ilhádaf min ilguwánti da ʔinn innās iṭṭúrš(ə) yiʔdáru yitkallímu má3a ʔayyə ḫadd(ə) min ɣēr mutárgim.*
6. *ilguwánti biytárgim ṣaḫḫ(ə) bi-nísbit tís3a w(i) tis3īn fi -lmíyya.*
7. *ilguwánti kamān biyíʔra ta3birāt ilwíšš.*
8. *ilbaḫisīn ílli 3ámalu -lguwánti biyʔūlu ʔinn ittiknulužyāt ittánya ílli bittárgim lúɣit ilʔišāra (i)lʔamrikíyya (t)iʔīla wi miš murīḫa, lākin ilguwánti da xafīf wi murīḫ.*
9. *munaẓẓámit iṣṣíḫḫa -l3alamíyya bitʔūl ʔinnə fī rub3umíyya sítta w(i) sittīn milyōn ʔáṭraš fi -l3ālam, wi nísba kibīra mínhum biyi3támidu 3ála lúɣit ilʔišāra.*

Translation of the Questions

1. How many deaf people are there in the world? 2. What is the purpose of these gloves? 3. Can the gloves read facial expressions? 4. What do you think about these gloves? 5. Do you think there are more deaf people nowadays? Why do you think that? 6. Do you know sign language? If so, how did you learn it? If not, would you like to? 7. Do you think that the whole world could someday speak the same language? Why? 8. Do you use any translation apps, such as Google Translate?

Answers to Expressions and Structures

1. American Sign Language لُغِةْ الإشارة الأمْريكية
2. the goal of these gloves الهدف مِن الجُوانْتي ده
3. translate correctly بِيْترْجِم صحّ
4. four hundred and sixty-six رُبْعُمية سِتّة و سِتّين

Notes

برجر كينج بيغير نظام أكل البقر

برجر كينج غير نظام أكل البقر في المزارع بتاعته و بيقول إن ده هيقلل انبعاثات الميثين اليومية بتاعتهم بحوالي ٣٣٪.

الشركة اشتغلت مع علماء من جامعتين عشان يعملوا نظام الأكل الجديد ده.

وكالة حماية البيئة (EPA) بتقول إن ٩.٩٪ من انبعاثات الميثين في أمريكا في ٢٠١٨ كانت من الزراعة. و أكتر من ربع الانبعاثات دي كانت من الحيوانات.

من سنتين، في ٢٠١٨، ماكدونالدز برضه قال إنهم بياخدوا خطوات عشان يقللوا انبعاثات الميثين و إنهم غيروا طريقة انتاج اللحمة في بعض السندوتشات.

برجر كينج و ماكدونالدز بدأوا برضه يحطوا خيارات أكل من غير لحمة على المنيوهات بتاعتهم.

برجر كينج بدأ يبيع برجر "الواپر اللي بينتج ميثين أقل" في عدد صغير من فروعه في أمريكا.

٢٣ Burger King Changes Cows' Diets

Key Words الكلمات

Study the key words and their definitions.

Translations	Definitions	Key Words
	نوْع الأكْل اللي شخْص أَوْ حَيَوان بِياكْلُه	نِظام أكْل (نُظُم أكْل)
	أشْهر حَيَوان بِياكُل عُشْب، بِناخُد مِنُّه لحْمة و لبن	بقرة (بقر)
	مكان كِبير الحَيَوانات بِتِترْبىّ فيه	مزْرعة (مزارِع)
	الغازات أَوْ الإشْعاعات اللي بِتُخْرُج مِن حاجة	اِنْبِعاثات
	بِيِحْصل كُلّ يوْم	يَوْمي
	هَيْئة بِتِعْمِل شُغْل بِالنِّيابة عن شخْص، مجْموعة، أَوْ شُغْل	وِكالة
	حركة لِقُدّام	خطْوَة (خطَوات)
	نقل حاجة في أَوْ على مكان أَوْ حاجة	حطّ (يِحُطّ)
	مكان صُغيرّ تابِع لِمكان كِبير	فَرْع (فُروع)

Now match these translations to the key words above. Check your answers in the answer key.

agency • branch • cow • daily • diet • emissions • farm • step • to put

1 **برْجر كينْج** بِيْغيرّ نِظام أكْل البقر

2 **برْجر كينْج** غيرّ نِظام أكْل البقر في المزارِع بِتاعْتُه و بِيْقول إنّ ده هَيْقلِّل انْبعاثات الميثيْن اليَوْمية بِتاعِتْهُم بِحَوالي تلاتة و تلاتين في المية.

3 الشِّرْكة اِشْتغلِت معَ عُلماء مِن جامْعِتيْن عشان يِعْمِلوا نِظام الأكْل الجِديد ده.

4 وِكالِةْ حِمايِةْ البيئة (EPA) بِتْقول إنّ تِسْعة و تِسْعة مِن عشرة في المية مِن اِنْبعاثات الميثيْن في أمْريكا في ألْفيْن و تمانْتاشر كانِت مِن الزِّراعة.

5 و أكْتر مِن رُبْع الانْبِعاثات دي كانِت مِن الحَيَوانات.

6 مِن سنتيْن، في ألْفيْن و تمانْتاشر، **ماكْدونالْدْز** برْضُه قال إنُّهُم بِياخْدوا خطَوات عشان يِقلِّلوا اِنْبعاثات الميثيْن و إنُّهُم غيرّوا طريقِةْ اِنْتاج اللّحْمة في بعْض السّنْدِوتْشات.

7 **برْجر كينْج** و **ماكْدونالْدْز** بدأوا برْضُه يِحُطّوا خِيارات أكْل مِن غيْر لحْمة على المِنْيوهات بِتاعِتْهُم.

8 **برْجر كينْج** بدأ يِبيع برْجر "**الواپر** اللي بِيِنْتِج ميثيْن أقلّ" في عدد صُغيرّ مِن فُروعُه في أمْريكا.

أسئلة الفهم Comprehension Questions

١. **بُرْجر كينْج** غيرّ نِظام أكْل كُلّ البقر بتاعُه؟

٢. كُلّ انْبِعاثات الميثيْن في أمْريكا مِن الحَيَوانات؟

٣. **ماكْدونالْدْز** بدأ إمْتى ياخُد خطَوات عشان يِقلِّل مِن انْبِعاثات الميثيْن؟

أسئلة المناقشة Discussion Questions

٤. أيْه رأْيَك في الخبر ده؟

٥. بِتْحِبّ الوَجْبات السِّريعة؟ أيْه أكْلِتك المُفضّلة؟

٦. جرّبْت قبْل كِده تِغيرّ نِظام أكْلك؟ ليْه؟

٧. تِفْتِكِر النّاس المفْروض ياكْلوا لحْمة أقلّ؟

٨. أيْه هُوَّ مطْبخك المُفضّل (أكْتر بلد بِتْحِبّ أكْلها)؟

Expressions and Structures تعبيرات و تراكيب

Try to remember the Arabic expressions and structures from the article. Each English translation is followed by four choices, only one of which is correct. Refer back to the article to check your answers.

1. **on its farms**

   على المزارِع بِتاعِتْها
   في الزِّراعة بِتاعْتُه
   في المزارِع بِتاعْتُه
   على مزْراعْتُه

2. **[the company] worked with scientists**

   شغّلِت معَ عُلما
   اِشْتغلوا عُلما
   اِشْتغلِت معَ عُلما
   شغّلِت العُلما

3. **two years ago**

   مِن سِنين اِتْنينْ
   مِن سنتينْ
   قبْل اِتْنينْ سنة
   سنتينْ قبْلها

4. **[Burger King] started selling**

   بدأ يِبيع
   بدأ بيْبيع
   بدأ بيّاع
   بدأ باع

Answer Key and Translations

الإجابات والترجمات

Key Word Answers

diet نِظام أكْل • cow بقرة • farm مزْرعة • emissions اِنْبعاثات • daily يَوْمي • agency وِكالة • step خطْوَة • to put حطّ • branch فَرْع

Translation of the Article

1. **Burger King Changes Cows' Diets**
2. Burger King has changed the diet of cows on their farms and says that this will reduce their daily methane emissions by 33%.
3. The company worked with scientists from two universities to make that new diet.
4. The Environmental Protection Agency says that more than 9.9% of greenhouse gas emissions in the US in 2018 were from agriculture.
5. And more than a quarter of those emissions were from animals.
6. Two years ago, in 2018, McDonald's also said that they were taking steps to reduce methane emissions and that they had changed the method of meat production in some sandwiches.
7. Burger King and McDonald's have also started to put food options without meat on their menus.
8. Burger King started selling the Reduced Methane Emissions Beef Whopper burger in a small number of their {his} branches in the US.

Phonemic Transcription of the Article

1. *[Burger King] biyɣáyyar niẓām ʔakl ilbáʔar*
2. *[Burger King] ɣáyyar niẓām ʔakl ilbáʔar fi -lmazāri3 bitá3tu wi biyʔūl ʔinnə da hayʔállil inbi3asāt ilmitēn ilyawmíyya b(i)ta3íthum bi-ɦawāli talāta w(i) talatīn fi -lmíyya.*
3. *iššírka (i)štáɣalit má3a 3ulamāʔ min gam3itēn 3ašān yi3mílu n(i)ẓām ilʔákl ilgidīd da.*
4. *wikālit ɦimāyit ilbīʔa ([EPA]) bitʔūl ʔinnə tís3a w(i) tís3a min 3ášara fi -lmíyya min inbi3asāt ilmitēn fi ʔamrīka f(i) ʔalfēn wi tamantāšar kānit min izzirā3a.*

5. *wi ʔáktar min rub3 ilʔinbi3asāt di kānit min ilḫayawanāt.*
6. *min sanatēn, fi ʔalfēn wi tamantāšar, [McDonald's] bárḍu ʔāl ʔinnúhum biyáxdu xaṭawāt 3ašān yiʔallílu (i)nbi3asāt ilmiṫēn w ʔinnúhum ɣayyáru ṭarīʔit intāg illáḫma fi ba3ḍ issandiwitšāt.*
7. *[Burger King] wi [McDonald's] bádaʔu bárḍu y(i)ḫúṭṭu xiyarāt ʔaklə min ɣēr láḫma 3ála -lminyuhāt bita3íthum.*
8. *[Burger King] bádaʔ yibī3 búrgar "il[Whopper] ílli biyíntig miṫēn ʔaʔáll" fi 3ádad ṣuɣáyyar min furū3u f(i) ʔamrīka.*

Translation of the Questions

1. Did Burger King change the diet of all of its cows? 2. Are all methane emissions in the US from animals? 3. When did McDonald's start taking steps to reduce methane emissions? 4. What is your opinion of this news? 5. Do you like fast food? What is your favorite food? 6. Have you tried changing your diet before? Why? 7. Do you think people should eat less meat? 8. What is your favorite cuisine (the country whose food you like best)?

Answers to Expressions and Structures

1. on its farms في المزارِع بتاعْتُه
2. worked with scientists اِشْتغلِت مع عُلما
3. two years ago مِن سنتينْ
4. started selling بدأ يبِيع

Notes

ممكن تجرب الـ"كورونا برجر"؟

"إحنا عندنا نكتة بتقول: لو خايف من حاجة، كلها!" دي نصيحة هوانج تونج، اللي بيشتغل طباخ في هانوي، ڤيتنام. تونج بدأ يبيع برجر على شكل ڤيرس كورونا.

العيش بتاع البرجر بيتحط له لون أخضر طبيعي. تونج بيقول: "إحنا بنحاول نخلي شكل الكورونا برجر ده حلو و كيوت." هو مش عايز الناس يخافوا و هما بيتكلموا عن الكورونا.

مطعم بيتزا هوم بتاع تونج بقى بيبيع حوالي ٥٠ كورونا برجر في اليوم، و المبيعات بتاعته زادت ٥٪. محلات و شركات كتير في هانوي كان لازم يقفلوا، بس بيتزا هوم و مطاعم تانية فضلوا فاتحين.

عدد سكان ڤيتنام أكتر من ٩٥ مليون. لحد النهارده (٢٠٢٠/١٠/١٨) مفيش في ڤيتنام غير حوالي ١١٢٦ حالة كورونا معروفة.

Would You Try the 'Coronaburger'?

Key Words — الكلمات

Study the key words and their definitions.

Translations	Definitions	Key Words
______________	حاجة مِش حقيقية بِتِتْقال عشان تِضحّك	نُكْتة (نُكت)
______________	حاجة بِتِتْقال عشان تِساعِد حدّ	نصيحة (نصايِح)
______________	المبْني لِلمجْهول مِن "حطّ"	اِتْحطّ (يِتْحطّ)
______________	اِسْتمرّ	فِضِل (يِفْضل)
______________	مفْتوح؛ مِش مقْفول	فاتِح
______________	نموذج	حالة
______________	إسْم مفْعول مِن "عِرِف"	معْروف

Now match these translations to the key words above. Check your answers in the answer key.

advice • case • joke • known • open • to be put • to remain

The Article المقالة

1 مُمْكِن تِجرّب الـ"**كوروْنا بُرْجر**"؟

2 "إحْنا عنْدِنا نُكْتة بِتْقول: لَوْ خايِف مِن حاجة، كُلْها."

3 دي نصيحِةْ **هْوانْج تونْج**، اللي بِيِشْتغِل طبّاخ في **هانوْي**، ڤيتْنام.

4 **تونْج** بدأ يِبيع بُرْجر على شكْل ڤَيْرس كوروْنا.

5 العيْش بِتاع البرْجر بِيِتْحطّ لُه لوْن أخْضر طبيعي.

6 **تونْج** بِيْقول: "إحْنا بِنْحاوِل نِخلّي شكْل **الكوروْنا بُرْجر** ده حِلْو و كْيوت."

7 هُوَّ مِش عايِز النّاس يِخافوا و هُمّا بِيِتْكلِّموا عن الكوروْنا.

8 مطْعم **بيتْزا هوْم** بِتاع **تونْج** بقى بِيْبيع حَوالي خمْسين **كوروْنا بُرْجر** في
اليوْم،

9 و المبيعات بِتاعْتُه زادِت خمْسة في المية.

10 محلّات و شرِكات كتِير في **هانوْي** كان لازِم يِقْفِلوا،

11 بسّ **بيتْزا هوْم** و مطاعِم تانْيَة فِضْلوا فاتْحين.

12 عدد سُكّان ڤيتْنام أكْتر مِن خمْسة و تِسْعين مِلْيوْن.

13 لِحدّ النّهارْده (تمانْتاشر، عشرة، عِشْرين عِشْرين) مفيش في ڤيتْنام غيْر
حَوالي ألف مية سِتّة و عِشْرين حالةْ كوروْنا معْروفة.

أسئلة الفهم Comprehension Questions

١. النُّكْتة في ڤيتْنام بِتْقول: 'لَوْ خايِف مِن حاجة متْاكُلْهاش'؟

٢. عدد سُكّان ڤيتْنام كام؟

٣. **تونْج** بِيْحاوِل يِخلّي شكْل **الكوروْنا بُرْجر** وِحِش؟

أسئلة المناقشة Discussion Questions

٤. أيْه رأْيَك في الكوروْنا بُرْجر؟

٥. عملْت أيْه في فترْةْ الحجْر في عِشْرين عِشْرين؟

٦. تِعْرف أيْه عن ڤيتْنام؟

٧. أيْه أحْسن نصيحة أخدْتها في حَياتك؟

٨. مين أحْسن حدّ تِعْرفْه بيِعْرف يِقول نُكت؟

Expressions and Structures تعبيرات و تراكيب

Try to remember the Arabic expressions and structures from the article. Each English translation is followed by four choices, only one of which is correct. Refer back to the article to check your answers.

1. **in the shape of the coronavirus**

جُوّه شكْل الكوروْنا ڤَيْرس — على شكْل ڤَيْرس كوروْنا

في الشّكْل مِن كوروْنا ڤَيْرس — في شكْل ڤَيْرس كوروْنا

2. **[he] does not want people to be afraid**

مُش عايِز إنّ النّاس يِخاف — ما عايِز النّاس يِخافوا

معايِزْش النّاس كانوا خايْفين — مِش عايِز النّاس يِخافوا

3. **[the restaurant sells] fifty burgers a day**

خمْسين بُرْجرات في اليوْم — خمْسين البرْجر اليَوْمي

خمْسين بُرْجر في اليوْم — الخمْسين بُرْجر يَوْمِيّاً

4. **there are only...**

بسّ فيه — مفيش بسّ

فيه غيْر — مفيش غيْر

Answer Key and Translations

الإجابات و الترجمات

Key Word Answers

joke نُكْتة • advice نصيحة • to be put اِتْحطّ • to remain فِضِل • open فاتح • case حالة • known معْروف

Translation of the Article

1. **Would You Try the 'Coronaburger'?**
2. "We have a joke that goes, 'if you're scared of something, eat it!'"
3. This is the advice of Hoang Tung, who works as a cook in Hanoi, Vietnam.
4. Tung started to sell burgers in the shape of the coronavirus.
5. The burger bun {bread} takes {is put to it} a natural green color.
6. "We try to make {the shape of} this Coronaburger look pretty and cute," Tung says.
7. He does not want people to feel scared when they talk about the coronavirus.
8. Tung's restaurant, Pizza Home, has been selling about 50 Coronaburgers per day,
9. and sales have increased by 5%.
10. Many shops and companies in Hanoi had to close,
11. but Pizza Home and other restaurants remained open.
12. The population {number of residents} of Vietnam is more than 95 million.
13. As of today, 10/18/2020, there are in Vietnam only {there aren't in Vietnam but} around 1126 known coronavirus cases.

Phonemic Transcription of the Article

1. *múmkin tigárrab il-"[Coronaburger]"?*
2. *íḫna 3andína núkta bitʔūl: law xāyif min ḫāga, kúlha!*
3. *di naṣīḫit [Hoang Tung], ílli biyištáɣal ṭabbāx fi hanōy, vitnām.*
4. *[Tung] bádaʔ yibī3 búrgar 3ála šakl váyras kurōna.*
5. *il3ēš bitā3 ilbúrgar biyitḫaṭṭə lu lōn ʔáxḍar ṭabī3i.*
6. *[Tung] biyʔūl: "íḫna binḫāwil nixálli šakl il[Coronaburger] da ḫilwə wi kyūt"*
7. *húwwa miš 3āyiz innās yixāfu, wi húmma b(i)yitkallímu 3an ilkurōna.*

8. *máṭ3am [Pizza Home] bitā3 [Tung] báda? biybī3 ɦawāli xamsīn [Coronaburger] fi -lyōm,*
9. *w ilmabi3āt bitá3tu zādit xámsa fi -lmíyya.*
10. *maɦallāt wi šarikāt kitīr fi hanōy kān lāzim yi?fílu,*
11. *bassə [Pizza Home] wi maṭā3im tánya fíd̦lu fatɦīn.*
12. *3ádad sukkān vitnām ?áktar min xámsa w(i) tis3īn milyōn.*
13. *li-ɦadd innahárda (tamantāšar, 3ášara, 3išrīn 3išrīn) ma-fīš fi vitnām ɣēr ɦawāli ?álfə míyya sítta w(i) 3išrīn ɦālit kurōna ma3rūfa.*

Translation of the Questions

1. Does the joke in Vietnam go, "If you're afraid of something, don't eat it?" 2. What is the population of Vietnam? 3. Does Tung try to make the Coronaburger look bad? 4. What do you think of the Coronaburger? 5. What did you do during quarantine in 2020? 6. What do you know about Vietnam? 7. What is the best advice you've ever gotten? 8. Who do you know that is the best at telling jokes?

Answers to Expressions and Structures

1. in the shape of the coronavirus على شكْل ڤَيْرس كورونا
2. does not want people to be afraid مِش عايِز النّاس يِخافوا
3. fifty burgers a day خمْسين بُرْجر في اليوْم
4. there are only... مفيش غيْر

Notes

دراسة: الأمريكان الأغنيا بيناموا أحسن من الفقرا

فيه دراسة أمريكية لقت إن الأمريكان الأغنيا بيناموا أكتر من الفقرا.

الدراسة عملت إحصائية على ١٤٠ ألف شخص، و لقت إن كل ما الواحد بيبقى أغنى، كل ما غالبا بينام أحسن بالليل.

خط الفقر في أمريكا دلوقتي ١٢,٧٦٠ دولار للشخص في السنة.

طبقا للأرقام الرسمية في أمريكا، حوالي ١٢.٥٪ من الأمريكان كانوا عايشين في فقر في ٢٠١٧.

الدكاترة بينصحوا بالنوم ٧ ساعات في اليوم. ٥٥٪ من الفقرا بيناموا ٧ ساعات في اليوم.

الدراسة مقالتش ده سببه أيه، لكن ممكن عشان الأغنيا بيقدروا يناموا في أماكن هادية و يروحوا للدكتور لما يمرضوا.

فيه دراسات تانية لقت إن النوم الوحش ممكن يعمل مشاكل صحية زي السمنة و أمراض القلب و السكر.

Study: Rich Americans Sleep Better Than Poor Ones

Key Words — الكلمات

Study the key words and their definitions.

Translations	Definitions	Key Words
	الحدّ الأدْنى مِن الفِلوس اللي الإنْسان بيِحْتاجُه عشان يأمِّن أساسيات المعيشة	**خطّ الفقْر**
	مُعْتمد مِن الحُكومة	**رسْمي**
	إدّى نصيحة	**نصح (ينْصح)**
	إجابةْ "ليْه؟"	**سبب (أسْباب)**
	مُشْكِلة صِحّية	**مرض (أمْراض)**
	جالُه مُشْكِلة صِحّية	**مِرِض (يمْرض)**
	زِيادةْ الوَزْن	**السِّمْنة**
	مرض بيْخلّي مُسْتَوى السُّكّر في الدمّ عالي	**السُّكّر**

Now match these translations to the key words above. Check your answers in the answer key.

diabetes • disease • obesity • official • poverty line • reason • to fall ill • to recommend, advise

The Article المقالة

1 دِراسة: الأمْريكان الأغْنِيا بِيْناموا أحْسن مِن الفُقرا

2 فيه دِراسة أمْريكية لقِت إنّ الأمْريكان الأغْنِيا بِيْناموا أكْتر مِن الفُقرا.

3 الدِّراسة عملِت إحْصائيِة على مية و أرْبعين ألْف شخْص، و لقِت إنّ كُلّ ما الواحِد بيِبْقى أغْنى، كُلّ ما غالِباً بِيْنام أحْسن بِاللّيْل.

4 خطّ الفقْر في أمْريكا دِلْوَقْتي اِتْناشر ألْف سُبْعُمية و ستّين دولار لِلشّخْص في السّنة.

5 طِبْقاً لِلأرْقام الرّسْمية في أمْريكا، حَوالي اِتْناشر و نُصّ في المية مِن الأمْريكان كانوا عايْشين في فقْر في ألْفيْن و سبعْتاشر.

6 الدّكاتْرة بيِنْصحوا بِالنّوْم سبع ساعات في اليوْم.

7 خمْسة و خمْسين في المية مِن الفُقرا بِيْناموا سبع ساعات في اليوْم.

8 الدِّراسة مقالِتْش ده سببُه أيْه، لكِن مُمْكِن عشان الأغْنِيا بيِقْدروا يِناموا في أماكِن هادْيَة و يِروحوا لِلدُّكْتور لمّا يِمْرضوا.

9 فيه دِراسات تانْيَة لقِت إنّ النّوْم الوِحِش مُمْكِن يِعْمِل مشاكِل صِحّية زيّ السِّمْنة و أمْراض القلْب و السُّكّر.

أسئلة الفهم Comprehension Questions

١. الدّكاتْرة بيِنْصحوا بِكام ساعة نوْم؟

٢. النّوْم الوِحِش مُمْكِن يِعْمِل أيْه؟

٣. الدِّراسة عملِت إحْصائيّة على كام شخْص؟

أسئلة المناقشة Discussion Questions

٤. أيْه رأْيَك في الدِّراسة دي؟ تِفْتِكِر ليْه الأغْنِيا بيِناموا أحْسن؟

٥. بِتْنام كام ساعة في اليوْم؟ بِتْنام أيّام الأجازة أكْتر مِن أيّام الشُّغْل؟

٦. هل عادات نوْمك اِخْتلفِت دِلْوَقْتي عن زمان؟

٧. تِفْتِكِر نِسْبِةْ الفُقرا قدّ أيْه في بلدك؟

٨. تِفْتِكِر مُمْكِن كُلّ النّاس في العالم يِكونوا أغْنِيا؟ ليْه؟

Expressions and Structures تعبيرات و تراكيب

Try to remember the Arabic expressions and structures from the article. Each English translation is followed by four choices, only one of which is correct. Refer back to the article to check your answers.

1. **a study found that...**

فيه دِراسات لقِت إنّ | فيه دِراسة لقِت إنّ

الدِّراسة لقِت إنّ | دِراسة لقِت فيها إنّ

2. **per capita annually**

لِلشّخْص لِلسّنة | لِلشّخْص في السّنة

شخْصاً سنَوِيّاً | في الشّخْص في السّنة

3. **it may be because...**

مِن المُمْكِن بِالسّبب | مِن مُمْكِن عشان

مُمْكِن يِكون السّبب | مُمْكِن عشان

4. **poor(-quality) sleep**

النّوْم الوحِش | وِحِش النّوْم

نوْم الفُقرا | النّوْم الفقير

Answer Key and Translations

الإجابات و الترجمات

Key Word Answers

poverty line خطّ الفقْر • official رسْمي • to recommend, advise نصح • reason سبب • disease مرض • to fall ill مِرِض • obesity السِّمْنة • diabetes السُّكّر

Translation of the Article

1. **Study: Rich Americans Sleep Better Than Poor Ones**
2. {There is} an American study [that] found that rich Americans sleep more than the poor ones.
3. The study surveyed 140,000 people and found that the richer a person becomes, the more likely they are to sleep better.
4. The poverty line in the US is now $12,760 per capita {for the person} a year.
5. According to {the} official numbers in the US, 12.3% of Americans were living in poverty in 2017.
6. Doctors recommend sleeping seven hours per day.
7. Fifty-five percent of poor people sleep seven hours per day.
8. The study did not say what the reason for this is, but it may be because the rich can sleep in quiet places and go to the doctor when they fall ill.
9. Other studies have found that poor-quality {bad} sleep can cause {make} health problems like obesity, heart disease{s}, and diabetes.

Phonemic Transcription of the Article

1. *dirāsa: ilʔamrikān ilʔaɣníya biynāmu ʔáħsan min ilfúʔara*
2. *fī d(i)rāsa ʔamrikíyya láʔit ʔinn ilʔamrikān ilʔaɣníya biynāmu ʔáktar min ilfúʔara.*
3. *iddirāsa 3ámalit iħṣaʔíyya 3ála míyya w(i) ʔarbi3īn ʔalfə šaxṣ, wi láʔit ʔinnə kullə ma -lwāħid biyíbʔa ʔáɣna, kullə ma ɣālíban biynām ʔáħsan bi-llēl.*
4. *xaṭṭ ilfáʔr(ə) f(i) ʔamrīka dilwáʔti (i)tnāšar ʔalf(ə) sub3umíyya w(i) sittīn dulār li-ššaxṣ(ə) fi -ssána.*
5. *ṭibqán li-lʔarqām irrasmíyya fi ʔamrīka, ħawāli (i)tnāšar wi nuṣṣə fi -lmíyya min ilʔamrikān kānu 3ayšīn fi faʔr(ə) fi ʔalfēn wi saba3tāšar.*

6. *iddakátra b(i)yinṣáħu bi-nnōm sába3 sa3āt fi -lyōm.*
7. *xámsa w(i) xamsīn fi -lmíyya min ilfúʔara biynāmu sába3 sa3āt fi -lyōm.*
8. *iddirāsa ma-ʔālitšə da sábabu ʔē, lākin múmkin 3ašān ilʔaɣníya b(i)yiʔdáru y(i)nāmu fi ʔamākin hádya wi y(i)rūħu li-dduktūr lámma yimráḍu.*
9. *fī dirasāt tánya láʔit ʔinn innōm ilwíħiš múmkin yí3mil mašākil ṣiħħíyya zayy issímna w(i) ʔamrāḍ ilʔálbə w issúkkar.*

Translation of the Questions

1. How many hours of sleep do doctors recommend? 2. What can poor {bad} sleep cause? 3. How many people did the study survey? 4. What do you think of this study? Why do you think the rich sleep better? 5. How many hours do you sleep a night {a day}? Do you sleep more on weekends than on work days? 6. Are your sleep habits different now than they used to be? 7. What do you think is the percentage of poor people in your country? 8. Do you think everyone in the world could be rich? Why?

Answers to Expressions and Structures

1. a study found that... فيه دِراسة لقِت إنّ
2. per capita annually لِلشّخْص في السّنة
3. it may be because... مُمْكِن عشان
4. poor(-quality) sleep النّوْم الوِحِش

Notes

الحر الرهيب و الجفاف بيزودوا الحرايق الطبيعية في كاليفورنيا

فيه حرايق طبيعية كتير بتحصل دلوقتي في كاليفورنيا. الحر الرهيب و الهوا الشديد و الجفاف بيزودوا الطين بلة.

اتنين من أكبر تلات حرايق في تاريخ الولاية بيولعوا حاليا، و ١٤ ألف رجل مطافي بيكافحوا الحرايق دي.

سبتمبر و أكتوبر عادة بيكونوا موسم للحرايق الطبيعية، بس السنة دي، اتسجل رقم قياسي جديد: حوالي ٨٠٠٠ كيلومتر مربع اتحرقوا.

المسؤولين بيقولوا إن السبب في زيادة الحرايق هو خطوط الكهربا و الهوا الشديد و الجفاف. فا لتجنب حرايق طبيعية جديدة، الكهربا اتقطعت عن أكتر من ١٧٠ ألف بيت في الولاية.

فيه متخصصين بيقولوا إن الوضع خطير جدا و لازم يتاخد بجدية.

كاليفورنيا اتعرضت لموجة حر شديدة في أجازة عيد العمال. درجة الحرارة وصلت ٣٨° في أماكن كتير في الولاية.

أماكن تانية في أمريكا برضه اتعرضت لتغيرات في الجو، زي دنفر كولورادو.

٣٥ Extreme Heat, Dry Weather Increase Wildfires in California

Key Words الكلمات

Study the key words and their definitions.

Translations	Definitions	Key Words
	مُتطرِّف	**رهيب**
	قَوي	**شِديد (شُداد)**
	عكْس "رُطوبة"	**جفاف**
	خلّى حاجة أَوْحش	**زوِّد (يِزوِّد) الطِّين بلّة**
	طلّع نار	**ولِع (يِوْلع)**
	دِلْوَقْتي	**حالِيّاً**
	حارِب	**كافِح (يِكافِح)**
	إنّك تِعْمِل أَوْ متِعْمِلْش حاجة عشان حاجة تانْيَة متِحْصلْش	**تجنُّب**
	المبْني لِلمجْهول مِن "قطع"	**اِتْقطع (يِتْقِطِع)**

Now match these translations to the key words above. Check your answers in the answer key.

avoidance • currently • dry weather {dryness} • extreme • strong • to battle, fight • to be cut • to burn (intransitive) • to make things worse {add wetness to mud}

1 الحرّ الرّهيب و الجفاف بِيْزوّدوا الحرايِق الطّبيعية في **كاليفورْنيا**

2 فيه حرايِق طبيعية كِتير بِتِحْصل دِلْوَقْتي في **كاليفورْنيا**.

3 الحرّ الرّهيب و الهَوا الشّديد و الجفاف بِيْزوّدوا الطّين بلّة.

4 اِتْنيْن مِن أكْبر تلات حرايِق في تاريخ الوِلايَة بِيوْلعوا حالِيّاً،

5 و أرْبعْتاشر ألْف رجْل مطافي بِيْكافْحوا الحرايِق دي.

6 سِبْتمْبِر و أُكْتوْبِر عادةً بِيْكونوا موسِم لِلحرايِق الطّبيعية،

7 بسّ السّنة دي، اِتْسجِّل رقْم قِياسي جِديد: حَوالي تمانْتلاف كيلومِتْر مُربّع اِتْحرقوا.

8 المسْؤولين بِيْقولوا إنّ السّبب في زِيادِةْ الحرايِق هُوَّ خُطوط الكهْربا و الهَوا الشّديد و الجفاف.

9 فا لِتجنُّب حرايِق طبيعية جِديدة، الكهْربا اِتْقطعِت عن أكْتر مِن مية و سبْعين ألْف بيْت في الوِلايَة.

10 فيه مُتخصّصين بِيْقولوا إنّ الوَضْع خطير جدّاً و لازِم يِتّاخِد بِجِدّية.

11 **كاليفورْنيا** اِتْعرّضِت لِموْجِةْ حرّ شِديدة في أجازِةْ عيد العُمّال.

12 درجِةْ الحرارة وِصْلِت تمانْيَة و تلاتين درجة مِئوية في أماكِن كِتير في الوِلايَة.

13 أماكِن تانْيَة في أمْريكا برْضُه اِتْعرّضِت لِتغيُّرات في الجوّ، زيّ **دِنْفر، كولورادو**.

أسئلة الفهم Comprehension Questions

١. أيْه سبب زِيادةْ الحرايِق الطّبيعية في **كاليفورْنِيا**؟

٢. الماَيّة اِتْقطعِت لِتجنُّب حرايِق طبيعية جِديدة؟

٣. الجوّ اِتْغير في أمريكا في **كاليفورْنِيا** بسّ. صحّ وَلّا غلط؟

أسئلة المناقشة Discussion Questions

٤. أيْه رأْيَك في الوَضْع في **كاليفورْنِيا**؟

٥. تِفْتكِر أيْه هِيَّ الصُّعوبات اللي رِجال المطافي بِيْواجْهوها؟

٦. فيه حرايِق طبيعية بِتِحْصل في بلدك؟ تِفْتكِر أيْه السّبب؟

٧. لَوْ كُنْت حاكِم **كاليفورْنِيا**، هتِعْمِل أيْه عشان تِحِلّ مُشْكِلةْ زِيادةْ الحرايِق الطّبيعية؟

٨. لَوْ هتْعيش في أمْريكا، هتِخْتار تِعيش فينْ؟ و ليْه؟

Expressions and Structures تعبيرات و تراكيب

Try to remember the Arabic expressions and structures from the article. Each English translation is followed by four choices, only one of which is correct. Refer back to the article to check your answers.

1. **two of the three biggest fires**

حريقينْ مِن تلات حرايِق أكْبر

اِتْنينْ مِن تلاتة أكْبر حرايِق

اِتْنينْ مِن أكْبر تلات حرايِق

اِتْنينْ في تلاتة مِن أكْبر حرايِق

2. **this year**

في السّنة ده

السّنة دي

دي السّنة

السّنة حاليّاً

3. **needs to be taken seriously**

لازِم يتّاخِد بِجِدّية

لازِم يتّاخِد بِجِدّة

لازِم يتّاخِد جِدّي

لازِم يتّاخِد جِدّاً

4. **other places**

أماكِن مُخْتلِفة

فيه مكان تاني

أماكِن تانْية

مكان مِن الأماكِن

Answer Key and Translations

الإجابات والترجمات

Key Word Answers

extreme رهيب • strong شِديد • dry weather جفاف • to make things worse زوِّد الطّين بلّة • to burn ولِع • currently حاليًّا • to battle, fight كافح • avoidance تجنُّب • to be cut اِتْقطع

Translation of the Article

1. **Extreme Heat, Dry Weather Increase Wildfires in California**
2. {There are} many wildfires [that] are occurring now in California.
3. The extreme heat, strong wind, and dry weather {dryness} make things worse.
4. Two of the three biggest wildfires in the state's history are currently burning,
5. and 14,000 firefighters are battling these wildfires.
6. September and October are usually wildfire season.
7. But this year, a new record was recorded: around 8,000 square kilometers have burned.
8. Officials say that the cause of {in} the wildfires are electricity lines, strong wind, and the dry weather {dryness}.
9. So, to avoid {for the avoidance of} new wildfires, electricity was cut from more than 170,000 homes in the state.
10. {There are} experts [who] say that the situation is so dangerous and has to be taken seriously.
11. California faced {was exposed to} a strong heatwave during the Labor Day {the holiday of workers} holiday.
12. The temperature has reached 38°C in many places in the state.
13. Other places in the US {America} also faced {were exposed to} changes in the climate, such as Denver, Colorado.

Phonemic Transcription of the Article

1. *ilɧárr irrahīb w ilgafāf biyzawwídu -lɧarāyiʔ iţţabi3íyya f(i) kalifúrniya*
2. *fī ɧarāyiʔ ţabi3íyya k(i)tīr bitíɧşal dilwáʔti f(i) kalifúrniya.*
3. *ilɧárr irrahīb w ilháwa -ššidīd w ilgafāf biyzawwídu -ţţīn bálla.*
4. *itnēn min ʔákbar tálat ɧarāyiʔ fi tarīx ilwilāya b(i)yiwlá3u ɧalíyyan,*

5. *wi ʔarba3tāšar ʔalfə rágul maṭāfi biykáfḫu -lḫarāyiʔ di.*
6. *sibtámbir wi ʔuktōbir 3ādatan biykūnu mūsim li-lḫarāyiʔ iṭṭabi3íyya,*
7. *bass issanādi, itsággil ráqam qiyāsi g(i)dīd: ḫawāli tamantalāf kilūmitrə murábba3 itḫáraʔu.*
8. *ilmasʔulīn biyʔūlu ʔinn issábab fi ziyādit ilḫarāyiʔ húwwa xuṭūṭ ilkahrába w ilháwa -ššidīd w ilgafāf.*
9. *fa li-tagánnub ḫarāyiʔ ṭabi3íyya g(i)dīda, ilkahrába itʔáṭa3it 3an ʔáktar min míyya wi sab3īn ʔalfə bēt fi -lwilāya.*
10. *fī mutaxaṣṣiṣīn biyʔūlu ʔinn ilwáḍ3ə xaṭīr gíddan wi lāzim yittāxid bi-giddíyya.*
11. *kalifúrniya (i)t3arráḍit li-mōgit ḫarr(ə) š(i)dīda f(i) ʔagāzit 3īd il3ummāl.*
12. *dáragit ilḫarāra wíṣlit tamánya w(i) talatīn dáraga miʔawíyya f(i) ʔamākin kitīr fi -lwilāya.*
13. *ʔamākin tánya f(i) ʔamrīka bárḍu (i)t3arráḍit li-taɣayyurāt fi -lgaww, zayyə [Denver], [Colorado].*

Translation of the Questions

1. What is the reason for the increase in wildfires in California? 2. Was water [supply] cut to avoid new wildfires? 3. In the US, the climate has changed in California only. True or false? 4. What do you think about the situation in California? 5. What challenges do you think firefighters {firemen} face? 6. Are there wildfires in your country? What do you think is the reason? 7. If you were the governor of California, what would you do to solve the problem of the increase in wildfires? 8. If you are going to live in the US, where would you choose to live? And why?

Answers to Expressions and Structures

1. two of the three biggest fires اِتْنينْ مِن أكْبر تلات حرايِق
2. this year السّنة دي
3. needs to be taken seriously لازِم يِتّاخِد بِجِدّية
4. other places أماكِن تانْيَة

Notes

CPSIA information can be obtained
at www.ICGtesting.com
Printed in the USA
BVHW042359060422
633601BV00015B/193